CAPTURING THE ... OF
A GROUP ... YAMERE
TAKING ON THE IMPOSSIBLE

Pioneering

—— In ——

Paris

BY LEAH THOMPSON

FORWARD BY JOE PORTALE

Hope you enjoy
the book!
♥ Leah Thompson

First Printing: 2018

ISBN - 978-0-244-13656-7

YWAM Paris Connect
5 rue de la Nouvelle France
Aubervilliers, 93300
France

For more information about YPC Publishing or about the book please contact:

info@ywamparisconnect.com

www.ywamparisconnect.com

Pioneering in Paris

by

Leah Thompson

Editors & Contributors
Kyla Shauer
Sarah Hastings
Chloe Brasington
Emily Mintz
Adam Thompson

YWAM Paris Connect

November 2018

This book is dedicated to our YWAM Perth and YWAM Biarritz Family. Without both of your support and friendship we would not be here.

TABLE OF CONTENTS

FOREWORD

Paris is one of the most visited cities in the world. What takes place in this world-class city strongly influences at least 50 nations in the French world and beyond. Youth With A Mission has been involved in a long-term battle for this city, to develop a major, international ministry and training center. Several teams have served faithfully there over the years, "cultivating faithfulness in the land."

We are excited about this renewed effort in Paris led by Adam and Leah Thompson and their team. God has given them unique giftings that are moving this work forward.

I have observed first-hand Adam and Leah's pioneering of their ministry in Paris over this past year. They have moved forward with a strong sense of faith as they have sought God and fought for every breakthrough that has taken place. They have persevered, moving from a personal vision of what God wanted, to the fulfillment of an international ministry and training center.

Today they are leading a growing community of Christians with a desire to minister to the heart of this great city. Their leadership of this Youth With A Mission ministry has been not only exciting but solid and consistent, with a clear grasp of the values of the mission. It has been a privilege to walk beside them at different points along the way, teaching in their Discipleship Training Schools and participating in the July outreach they led in the city.

On each occasion I have seen them lead with integrity, understanding and maturity. In this book Leah shares from her heart the amazing things God has done over this past year.

I highly recommend to you Adam and Leah, their ministry and this book. May God enlarge your faith as you read these stories of His faithfulness to this ministry and to this city.

Joe Portale

Founder,

YWAM French Ministries

INTRODUCTION

Victories only come after a massive amount of struggle. If there isn't that struggle then we wouldn't call them victories. They would just be nice events that happened. We would enjoy them and then quickly forget . When there's a victory, it comes usually after you have given everything of yourself, when you're bloody from war and are at the brink of losing hope and faith. This past year was exactly that for me. I felt like I was constantly going through a bloody war, living in the trenches and trying to survive.

I've always heard pioneering wasn't easy. I already knew it wasn't, but this was a whole other level of personal and corporate struggle that I had never been through before. My faith and trust in God was tested to a different degree than ever before. Through the trial and the trenches when I felt bloody and ready to give up, I knew I couldn't. I've learned enough that something always has to give. If it's a word of the Lord and God has spoken it then He is faithful to come through even though everything around you says He won't.

Darlene Cunningham, the co-founder of Youth With A Mission (YWAM) says that we need to be a "Do Not Quit" generation. I held onto that during this year, as hard as it was, I knew I did not want to be one that gave up. There will always be struggle in our lives. There will always be hard times, especially those of us who are called to forcefully advance the kingdom of God through missions in nations. What I've learned is to stay faithful to the word of God. Do not give up even though everything looks like it is failing, remain steadfast and trust in what God will do. This is what this year concreted in me even more so I have a greater foundation to stand on for when the next level of trusting comes.

The missionary life is not easy; You often feel you are in a battle and you're always fighting for something whether that is finances or accommodation or people or... But the end goal and the fruit of the fight is always worth it; it's always worth it. Whether it be ministering to homeless men to bring encouragement to their day and be a seed for them to find a way out or for the DTS student that comes and seeing them know God more. It is worth it. That's what I gladly give my life to.

God has been putting it on my heart and mind for a while to write books, which is absurd because I haven't been trained or had a strong desire to write. I mean I barely passed high school with a whole lot of Cs and not much care. I knew at the age of thirteen that I was going to be a missionary. I saw that as my way out of trying hard in school.

To my regret, I didn't apply myself or really even try. I tried at sports and did pretty well, but I do wish I was wholehearted in learning about spelling and grammar (especially now since God himself is asking me to write a book).

It's funny I know, but God is kind in his leading and persistent in His approach to moving me out of my comfort zone. In a comfort zone, there is safety and no risk, but there is also no growth. So here I go, stretching myself to grow and pour out the last year of my life into a book.

I look back now at this last year and I am amazed. I actually can't fully comprehend all that has happened. I didn't want the book to be that long, and I am sure people don't want to hear how God provided for my husband's favourite couch at a special deal.

As I began writing, I realized the amount of stories I could write were more than I could fit in the book. These stories are the ones that stood out to me and I hope they give clear understanding of our journey and how God has lead us this far. It wasn't all pretty, and this year was hard, but its blessings and encouragements along the way haven't been forgotten.

Paris was a big shift from Biarritz. Biarritz is a small gorgeous town in the Southwest of France that borders Spain, while Paris is an artistic city of millions of people and famous architect. In early 2009, I was on staff with YWAM Perth. God spoke to me that new vision was coming. Soon after I was approached by Daniel and Kate Appa to pioneer a YWAM base in Biarritz. I was in a place in my life that was ready for a change and an adventure with Jesus. So I was excited when God said yes to going.

Soon after announcing it to everyone, a young kiwi guy asked me out. I was shocked by this ask. He was two years younger than me, I had been leading him in the property and maintenance ministry, and I had staffed his Discipleship Training School. As I left that conversation and asked God about it, God said that this was good. So I said yes to start dating this young kiwi guy, Adam Thompson.

Adam was a popular guy at the YWAM base in Perth. He was funny, played guitar, and had a neat accent. I never really took notice of him, so I didn't realize he took notice of me. But as we started dating, I knew within the first week this was going somewhere. Adam was a man of integrity and one who feared the Lord. I myself was still committed to join the pioneering work in France with the Appas. Adam was committed to YWAM Perth for two more years. In this, I felt to delay my commitment to Biarritz so that we could move together. Adam and I married in 2010 and after two years in Perth we moved to Biarritz.

When we joined, there were five other staff members on base and a team on outreach. It was a big change for us, moving from YWAM Perth where there were over 300 people at any given time. It truly was a pioneering experience. The base was made up of four little apartments all together. When we arrived we found out that we would only be in these apartments for three months. Then we had to all find new places to live, and a new base to move into.

It was exciting and new for us. New language, new people, new surroundings. We absolutely loved it!

We were people who loved new adventures and new mission fields. We were well equipped in our previous YWAM years to know what we were getting into. Small but mighty was our little YWAM base in the south of France. We grew and developed quickly. We were soon asked to join the leadership team of the base. We were so humbled and encouraged by this and our personal growth and our capacities grew greatly.

Adam and I started to flourish and were taught well on how to lead. It was huge for us to spread our wings in ways that only a small base would provide. It was exhilarating! Our base in Biarritz grew quickly with three DTS's a year.

The base leader Daniel Appa is an exceptional leader and one of the most releasing leaders Adam and I have ever known. He shaped us in leadership more then we realized and through his mentorship we were able to make choices, make mistakes, and learn well. This truly trained and prepared us for pioneering our own base.

After five years in Biarritz, the word of the Lord came and we knew it was time to launch out into a new city and multiply. The word that was key for me to leave Perth was the same word that brought me to Paris:

"Listen to me, you who pursue righteousness and who seek the Lord. Look to the rock from which you were cut and to the quarry from which you were hewn" Isaiah 51:1 (NIV)

Through this verse God was speaking to me about taking the values from YWAM Perth and YWAM Biarritz and using it to form a new work. This, for me, was key in starting a new base and multiplying the same DNA into this city (with, of course, a Leah & Adam Thompson twist).

Our call was to impact the city of Paris and see transformation and change in France but also the world! Paris is the most visited city in the world and the opportunities to reach every nation through Paris is massive. God spoke to me one day that to "Save Paris" in turn would "Save the World." It was a huge statement. I was blown away by God saying that; it was his strategic eye on the city. That he wasn't just calling us to another big city but he was calling us to see change worldwide through this city. No matter where you go in the world people know about Paris or someone has an Eiffel Tower picture on a bag or journal or picture.

One time I was in Perth, Australia visiting a house and there was a big Eiffel Tower canvas on the wall. Paris is an influential city and God has something He is doing with this city.

God also gave me an image of Paris being like a bridge to the unreached nations, to places that have never heard the gospel. In the image, French people were coming from Paris and going to unreached people and a bridge was built between them. It was an image of missionaries going forth and some would plant long term works and some would go back and forth over the bridge from Paris to the unreached nations.

I also saw the unreached people coming to Paris as well and coming back over the bridge. It was a neat image of nations reaching nations. This city is on the heart of God. I love that we were in the midst of it.

OCTOBER

The Lord had said to Abram, "Go from your country, your people and your father's household to the land I will show you."

Genesis 12:1 (NIV)

We started our drive to Paris with our packed truck full of all of our belongings and everything we own. For Adam and I moving was not a new thing and being flexible with change was normal for us. We both have spent our adult lives as missionaries and knew to not hold tightly to possessions or personal space. We had been married for seven years and our home was in Biarritz, France for the last five years staffing and helping pioneer a YWAM work there.

It was incredible and we had made ourselves a home, but now we were leaving, driving away with a giant moving van and a team of twelve to start a new base in the most visited city of the world, Paris.

The city of Paris wasn't often on our hearts and mind over the first five years of living in France. It was funny to think we were moving there since it wasn't some deep desire or even a strong word from heaven written in the clouds to move there. It was simple words from the Lord and alignment of choices of obedience that directed and led us to the conclusion that Paris was what God was speaking to Adam and I.

Three years previous God gave me a download that one day Adam and I would potentially be planting a new work somewhere. I was thinking it was Bordeaux, another city in France, but that city never sat well with Adam and not really with myself either if I was being honest.

It wasn't until the end of March 2017 when Adam and I were on a trip in England for our seventh anniversary that the idea came. I remember it so well because we were staying at a nice hotel and my favourite thing about staying at a hotel is having the breakfast in the morning. This hotel had a beautiful English buffet breakfast. There was unlimited coffee and bacon and eggs and hash browns and even a whole salmon! I was in heaven.

So here we were having a wonderful breakfast together. I was on cloud nine and on my second round of bacon and eggs and focused on my meal when Adam turns to me suddenly. I saw how excited and expressive he was getting so I gave him my full attention.

"Ok," he said with his hands at his face, equally spread apart ready to declare something big to me. "I've been thinking and I felt God drop a city into my mind that I have been thinking about for a few days now."

I was surprised and excited because I have been feeling for a time that God was calling us out of Biarritz and I was waiting for God to speak to Adam as well and especially about where because we both didn't know.

Then Adam said with his hands still raised between his head, "What about Paris?"

I stopped, paused, reflected for thirty seconds and within that time I felt all the words I had for pioneering a base and everything God had been speaking to me just fell into complete alignment and all my words transferred completely to Paris.

I then replied, "Yes. Absolutely."

There wasn't any more discussion in my mind. I was set —
it made sense and within minutes the wet cement of the idea was
becoming hard concrete within me. Paris was the answer for all the
words and desires that God was speaking to us! It was perfect!
Adam and I love cities and love culture and many people and
various ministries and multiplication and big things and
movements! Paris was all these things! Any ministry and any
opportunity is possible within this city.

I think Adam was surprised by how quick I got on board
with it — but I was in. We both were. Paris would be our new
home.

We drove up with our giant moving truck and two other
vehicles, one was Adam and I's car and the other was our green
little Renault called BBG or Baby Groot. We had eleven of us
driving up with us but twelve on our team. The 12th member took a
train up earlier and was helping a friend in Paris with a concert the
first evening.

On our drive up we made two important stops along the
way; McDonalds for the five-euro Egg McMuffin breakfast and the

second was a rest stop where we had lunch. The rest stop was more of a memorable experience than the McDonalds breakfast, even though it was very good. At the lunch rest stop we sat together half way until our destination eating our squishy packed sandwiches from the morning.

The sandwiches were a bit soggy, but we were happy as there was so much adventure and unknowns ahead for us all. After we finished eating Adam led us in an act of remembrance were he asked each of us to go find a rock. We all ran around and found our rocks, different shapes and sizes. Some were as big and some were tiny. It was an interesting exercise to see what different people came back with.

We each held our rock and examined them and then one by one we explained why we picked our said rock. Each person had different meanings and depth to what God was speaking to them through their rock. It was a powerful exercise as it was personal word from God and how it then resonated to each one of us corporately.

One by one we shared and as we finished sharing we each put our rock in the middle of our picnic table and we started to build an altar. Throughout the scriptures it talks about building altars to the Lord and altars of remembrance so that is what we did. Building our altar of remembrance as we were halfway to Paris and about to step into starting a new YWAM base.

An altar of remembrance for us was twofold. One part was made to mark and remember how God has lead us this far and to remember His faithfulness to us. Secondly it was to give God thanksgiving and worship. We never wanted to think so highly of ourselves to forget all that God has done for us and all He will continue to do.

So building our altar of remembrance on our way to Paris was a significant marker for us to never forget where we came from and where we were going. It was a beautiful act and we prayed and gave thanksgiving to God for taking us on this journey and how He was leading us.

Once we finished we were rejuvenated and ready to get there. All of us had our fresh words from God and it caused our faith levels to rise and start what God was speaking to us! We drove for four more hours and made it to our first home in Paris in a city called Massy.

Massy is a city an hour south of Paris. It's a small city with not much in it, not much to do, and it's not a particularly nice place with lots of government funded apartments with families crammed into them. On our first day there, someone saw the police arrest a person. It wasn't quite oozing with culture and history like the touristic parts of Paris.

We had arranged with a Christian language school called Les Cedres that is based in Massy to stay in one of their apartments for one month. It was a huge answer to prayer as all of September we were searching for a place to live and could find nothing, but finally two weeks before we had to leave Biarritz Les Cedres said it would work for us to stay for a month! We were overjoyed.

It was a three bedroom apartment with a good size living room and kitchen. We were on the fifth floor of the apartment block with no elevator so our legs strengthened during that month from all the up and downs! In two bedrooms of the apartment we put two girls in one and three in the other. Adam and I took the third bedroom which was a good size room with a queen bed.

Then in Les Cedres facility across the street they gave us two of their dorm rooms at their centre so we could fit the rest of our staff. So the two boys went into one of those rooms and two more staff girls in the other. We were eleven in total for the first month with one staff who went on holidays for that month. Les Cedres also let us use their youth room for our office and meeting space for the month.

This was huge for us as we were starting out as a base and needed to get into systems and structure and having a space of our own was encouraging! From the apartment to the Les Cedres was only a three min walk so it all worked out perfectly. We were becoming a real YWAM base.

The first week in Massy we set up cleaning rosters and jobs. two people to be in charge of the kitchen, one person on communications, one on media, one on accounts, one on legal documents, one on teaching French and four people learning beginners French, one on house hunting , etc. I was amazed at how quick we made our home a home and our base a base. It was awkward relationally as well because all eleven of us haven't all been in this situation before. Living together in an apartment and doing life so closely it took time to develop normality in it but when it did we had fun and joy came quickly with all our different personalities and quirks!

Our schedule was from Monday to Friday with weekends free. Monday, Tuesday, Thursday and Friday were normal schedules. We would start the day with half hour of cleaning the apartment, then we would do either worship or intercession then we would have two hours of either French learning or our various jobs. Then we would all have lunch together, family style and eat around the table. After Lunch we cleaned, took a break and then worked on our appointed tasks until dinner at 6:30pm. After dinner we would hang out, watch a movie or chill.

On Wednesdays of each week we went into Paris to the Champs de Mars to do worship, evangelism or bible reading.

Getting into Paris from Massy took about ninety minutes so we would make a day of it with packed lunches and head out in the morning until the late afternoon.

Each Wednesday felt a bit like the glory day of what was to come. Getting out of Massy to downtown Paris and to sit in front of the Eiffel Tower and read scripture and tell people about Jesus. This is what we came here to do!

So Wednesdays were a delight. On one Wednesday evangelism time we were on our break and having our packed lunches in front of Eiffey (my pet name for the Eiffel tower) and two homeless men came up to us to ask for money.

Immediately my spirit leaped and I said, "Silver and gold I do not have but what I have I will give to you, can I pray for you?"

The two men hesitated then said yes. They sat down and I proceeded to talk with them about their lives. They were from Eastern Europe and spoke English and were just trying to scrape by in life. I felt God was after these men. I started encouraging them and prayed for them. One of them just started crying, he knew about God and knew the truth and we encouraged him to return to Him. It was a beautiful time of loving on these sweet broken men that have gone through a lot. They soon left and went on their way and I again processed, *This is why I do what I do.*

In October we began our hunt for long term housing as well. We had Massy for one month and in November and December we had another short term rental house in a suburb called Bois-Colombes. But our need was a long term building as January was approaching and we would increase by thirty people quite rapidly.

So the hunt was on to find a house or building or something for us to have by January. Adam and I's dream was to have a big building that we can host hundreds of people with multi-function rooms for classrooms and a big kitchen and yard for people to come to, learn, be discipled, grow as leaders, and go to the nations to help and serve others.

Adam and I love community and love being able to provide a place of belonging for people and a healthy place to grow and develop and become the people God has called them to be. So when we prayed and asked God what to fight for in Paris, it was immediately about a large facility that we can function out of and be who we were called to be.

Youth With a Mission— to know God and make Him known—that is our mandate.

This is also Adam and my life's call—to train people up in the ways of God and then send them out to the nations and places to tell others about Jesus. We've both been a part of this mission for over ten years and we don't see ourselves doing anything different for the rest of our lives. So moving to Paris we knew it was a long term call of commitment to this city and to building a base.

We started looking for our ideal building and soon realized it was going to be quite the battle to get a large building. The costs to rent, or buy, a building in Paris were crazy prices and we soon sobered to the fact that this was all going to have to be a God thing, because we had no money. All of us were living month by month.

We didn't have enough to put down for a place. One place I found which in my mind was perfect size and location and had a big beautiful yard costs €75 million to buy! Of course I dreamed as I looked at the photos, but was thinking, *Ok God, you gotta do you because wow this is a lot to get our hands around.*

Before we left Biarritz I had read Isaiah 55 and felt God spoke to me about the building that we would get one day. We wanted to own something and not rent for too long because we want to make it our own and develop it for us as a base and community. So as I was reading the same chapter, and these words stood out to me.

"You who have no money, come, buy and eat! Come, buy wine and milk without money and without cost. Why spend money on what is not bread, and you labor on what does not satisfy? Listen, listen to me, and eat what is good, and you will delight in the richest of fare." Isaiah 55 (NIV)

As I read this I thought *yes, we have no money.* God was speaking a promise to me—*come and buy without money and without cost.*

For a building, he wanted to give us the best—and specifically to buy something without money or cost. He was saying not to worry about the money, even a sense that maybe one day someone may give us a building or buy a building for us.

It was a huge promise. And God was so clear to me about it—that we were going to delight one day in the richest of fare as a base. This brought so much encouragement to me. Even as I scrolled through the seventy five million dollar properties I knew God is so faithful to me and us and that seventy five million is just a number for Him. It's not even a hard number. He owns everything anyway.

So I allowed myself to dream in the process of finding a place for us because God had spoken about the best for us. I held on to that promise. So we looked at houses and contacted many real estate agents but nothing really moved forward in October. However, we were ok as we knew we had two more months in Bois-Colombes to find a place.

In Massey, we soon discovered that when you're faced with starting the base with eleven people that some people have money for staff fees and some do not. Of course we don't want anyone to go hungry. So we looked at our finances and provided food for what we could afford. As a base, we joined together to pray for finances.

Our base started with no income. All we had was what each staff had for that month's staff fees. We were all trusting together for the finances. Some of our staff had the full amount and some didn't. Our budget allowed four euros a day for food and ten euros a day for accommodation per person.

That was the budget that we had in Biarritz. When Adam and I talked about raising the fees because it's Paris, we didn't feel it was right. So we left it the same and stood in faith for God to provide the rest.

Four euros covers three meals a day. Breakfast is a simple meal of cereal or toast. Lunches and dinners were nice cooked meals. When we added up how much we had for our month of food for all of us it was half our budget. We were looking at working off of two euros a person per day.

We told the base the situation. Then said if we didn't see more finances come in, we would be all eating pasta with red sauce because it's the cheapest thing to make. We talked about it and made peace about it because we knew the call was worth it! Even if our food quality had to suffer a bit. We also looked at our finances in relation to putting a caution for the next house we were going to move into the next month. We needed €2500 to give to the owners. We didn't have that finance either.

So like any good YWAMer we had a prayer time. We gathered together as staff. I felt like God was challenging us to be generous with one another. So we asked the Lord together and as individuals how we can be generous.

Soon different ones had different ideas of how we can be generous with one another. We had a beautiful time of giving! One staff gave close the amount of the deposit of the next house we were moving into. Others felt to help pay needed staff fees. God told Adam and I to go to Pizza Hut and buy everyone lunch. It was also one of our staff's birthday that day. So we packed up and excitedly went to all-you-can eat pizza.

It's a beautiful kingdom principle that generosity breeds generosity. As you sew in generosity you reap of it. So we put that into practice. Soon, as a base, we saw release of finances and all that we needed to get us through the first month as a base. The best part about this was we never had to eat cheap spaghetti noodles and sauce. God in His kindness provided the whole way.

The other amazing thing that happened in October was that we legally became an official registered organization. Before we became a legal association in France, we were laughing because we were just a group of people meeting in an apartment. But when we became legal we all celebrated.

We weren't just a bunch of people meeting in a room anymore. We had the full label as an association in France called Jeunesse En Mission Paris Centrale, which is Youth With A Mission, Paris Central. Our first month as a base and an association was a success.

We were also able to bless and encourage Les Cedres with two worship evenings that Adam and a few of our staff lead. We finished off October with a deep breath of feeling accomplished.

But we were also ready for a change and a move to be closer to the city and closer to where God was calling us—Paris Central.

NOVEMBER

"I will give you every place where you set your foot...Be strong and

very courageous."

Joshua 1:3,7 (NIV)

The excitement to move to our new house closer to the city

was huge. After living an hour and a half away from the city for a

month, it was wearing on all of us. Especially because our heart

and vision was the city of Paris!

We were stoked with the move and ready for more space

and change. All twelve of us packed up our minimal supplies that

we had for one month and moved to a suburb in the west of greater

Pairs called Bois Colombes which means wood doves.

The house was gorgeous and private with its own gate and

parking spaces. We were on a quiet small little street and fall was

beginning to set in and all the leaves were either falling or changing

colours. It felt to satisfying to move into an actual house and a

more proper base than a squishy apartment where we felt we were

just a bunch of friends hanging out together all the time.

The house made YWAM Paris Central an official base for us. We became legit a "real" YWAM work. This was both encouraging and humbling to see how quick God had led us and how faithful he had been to provide good things.

The house was made of brick and had a main floor and two floors above it with a spacious basement as well. With six bedrooms we felt like kings. There was space and freedom to move around and to stop living on top of each other and to even get more items from our storage unit! The boys took the room on the left on the top floor. Adam and I took the room on the right. We also had one room available for any guests that would come our way.

Hospitality, value seventeen of our foundational values of YWAM, was a value that we wanted to be foundational for us as a base. Not soon after we arrived in Bois Colombes we had a lot of enquiries of different people with need for accommodation. We soon realized that starting a base in Paris means a lot of people come through this city are in need of a place to stay. It is a major hub for international flights. Plus, having over 20,000 YWAMers in the world traveling, this means a lot of people to host. Not that we said yes to everyone, but we tried to be as helpful and hospitable as we could. I loved it.

My heart is hospitality. Especially after spending a year working in that ministry in 2011 with YWAM Perth. Hospitality was something I grew to love and desired to be a part of who I am and who our base will be. It means more work, yes, and at times can be strenuous with space and answering lots of peoples questions and inquiries. But if we get to show Jesus to people by giving them a peaceful place to rest for an evening, then it is so worth the effort.

We put three girls in each room on the middle floor and then due to needing one more bed for a girl we squeezed Alice, our beautiful Aussie staff, in the office room which was only big enough to fit a single bed. The door barely closed, but with Alice to make it her home was easy and soon was decorated beautifully and used to the best of the ability as a tiny room can be. So all twelve of us settled in well and my heart was at rest.

I struggle with over responsibility and taking on the needs of others as my own. Yes, it can be an amiable quality having responsibility—but not at the expense of my own sanity. I was concerned that everyone liked their room and felt like they belonged. I became too concerned about them all. My worry was diminishing the reality that God is able to take care of our base and staff way better than I ever can. There comes a point where "caring" can become overbearing, controlling, and even self-focused rather than on the person.

We see it in parents not willing to let their kids go. I saw that I was going that way in my mind. I had to learn to take my hands off and turn off my brain. I knew that these were grown adults with a call of God on their lives. God is in charge of their lives. Not me.

I can release them to God and He will take care of them. He called them. He has them. No need for me to worry about them. I had to allow God to do His thing. After I learned that I was able to just be at peace more, rest on my days off, and learn not to worry as much.

Soon after moving into Bois Colombes we started a thirty-day fast and prayer on the first of November. We were on the hunt for a new permanent building as the January Backpack Europe DTS was quickly approaching and we were looking like we would have fifteen to twenty students. Then with more staff joining us the first few weeks of January, it meant we were looking for a house that would fit up to forty people.

It was a big leap from housing twelve people and that was hard enough to find so we felt God was leading us to fast and pray for the release of a building. We rotated two people fasting a day and each lunch they would pray for the release of a new building. Soon after we starting praying and fasting so many words came in about our new house...

Being a building with space and room.

The song "Big Big House" by Audio Adrenaline was on repeat in our prayers and conversations: "A big big house with lots and lots of rooms. A big big house with lots and lots of food. A big big house where we can play football. A big big house. It's my Father's house."

We loved it and asked for it. The promises and words kept coming through that God had good things for us and that the "Best is yet to Come." We kept hearing words of the house being one of family and community and space to be ourselves. To be loud and have worship and not worry about our neighbours complaining about the noise.

It was beautiful for all of us to be hearing God and dreaming with God about what the future of our little base would look like. We got excited as we shared our words and had times of worship and prayer together weekly. God was faithful in meeting with us daily and dreaming with us.

One day we had a word of the Widow's Oil from 2 Kings 4. Where she started pouring out the last of her oil and it filled all the jars that she had gathered. God spoke to us to gather jars and fill them up with what He wants to pour out! We asked the Lord what the jars should be. We filled a list of items from fluffy blankets to turkeys for Christmas to new iPhones for people who had old phones.

It was incredible and built a lot of faith in the twelve of us. We started praying and asking for these jars to be filled. We started contacting organizations for donations and writing different people and churches to put our *jars* out there to see if they could get filled. We moved in faith from what God was speaking. In obedience, we also went to local bakeries and supermarkets to ask for donations.

One day we sent a team out to go around to ask supermarkets and bakeries. They returned with one *yes* to come back later and pick up the free bread. We all were over the moon!

So that evening they went back to the bakery and came back with two giant bags of French pastries and bread. All for free! We danced and were so thrilled at God's provision. This bakery gave us free bread and pastries every day pretty much for the whole two months we were in Bois Colombes.

It was unreal. We had so much bread we didn't know what to do with it! The blessing, the abundance and the overflow was so incredible for us.

God was faithful with His word of the jars. Costco had sales on fluffy blankets and by the end of the year we all had a fluffy warm blanket. Finances came in for people to get new iPhones and even Microsoft approved us for getting deals on different products! We were amazed again at the faithfulness and the abundance of our God.

Through all the abundance the looming thought was always in the back of my mind, *When are you going to provide a house for us? For the DTS and for us as a base?*

Adam and I had been going to many houses and did a lot of research and one of our key staff Thierry Noamessi did a lot of phone calls to real estate agents. Thierry is originally from Ghana and was in staff with us for many years in Biarritz.

When he prayed and felt to come with us to Paris, Adam and I were both overjoyed as he is such a key asset to the team. He is fluent in both English and French and is a strength for us as he always gets the job done. Thierry made so many phone calls and we had so many negative responses as people were scared to rent to an organization. Not many people wanted a young Christian organization taking over their property. They also wanted more proof of finances—which we had only been a base for a month so that was quite hard to prove.

It was hard for me. The faith was there, but as the end of November was upon us I kept praying, "Please Lord, can we find one before Christmas so we can enjoy Christmas before we move."

Every time we prayed for our accommodation and for a home the promises of God and the words that were coming through were massive. All about a big house and space for us and good things. But day after day we kept hearing a no. Every meeting Adam and I had to go to we got dressed up fancy. We needed to look legit of course—so I did my hair, makeup, and put on my fancy jacket (that I got at a garage sale of course) and away we would go.

We met a lot of real estate agents and saw a lot of houses. Not many we liked and not many that would work. These meetings would also take such a long time because we had to drive everywhere and then find parking and pay for parking so it usually took the whole morning or day to do one or two meetings.

We were in faith, but it was also a journey of perseverance.

Adam soon had an idea that we needed to get a scooter. It meant free parking and it is easier to get around a city with a scooter than a car because you can zoom through traffic. I was not 100% convinced but was like, ok if God wants us to get a scooter then he will provide. Soon after we were at some a friend's house in the city and the mention of needing a scooter came up.

Our friend said, "Oh actually I have another scooter that I don't need you can have it!"

It was amazing! So all we had to do was buy a battery for it and Adam had to get the right license which only took him a few hours to do one morning. Just like that we got a scooter and were zooming around the city from meeting to meeting!

Even though we saw many houses and went to many meetings there was not one yes to us being able to rent a house for January. It was hard for us, for me, but we kept pushing forward and kept getting words of victory and "the best is yet to come."

November was full of prayer, fasting, more prayer, seeing houses and calling real estate agents and bible reading in Paris. We felt God say to read out the whole bible at Champs de Mars. So every Wednesday we would pack our lunches and go to Champs de Mars and split into teams and read out the scriptures there. We did that for November and December to speak truth of God's word over the land.

DECEMBER

"He brought me out into a spacious place; he rescued me because he delighted in me"

Psalm 18:19 (NIV)

December came upon us quickly in our quiet little world of Bois Colombes.

The first weekend we decorated the house with a Christmas tree and decorations that we dug out of storage. Immediately the atmosphere changed. We were children ready and counting down to the big day!

A word from one of our staff came through for all of us staff to trust for finances to get everyone a gift. We were only twelve people, so it wasn't that outrageous but enough to trust for an extra €100 or more of support to get good gifts for everyone. Everyone took that on as a word and soon shopping and present wrapping was under way! It was incredible the joy for generosity and making this a Christmas to remember.

We were all in a new situation and lifestyle. Family and community were key for us in creating the base that God wanted us to create.

It was amazing to see how God continually lead us in the month of December as we prayed and worshiped and kept trusting Him. Words kept coming through about the house and that God was going to do something big for us. I was in faith, but struggled with my own desires getting in the way.

I deeply wanted Christmas to be a time to be together, to relax and enjoy, before we moved again. Inevitably getting busy with the Backpack Europe DTS. So I was praying that we would have a house to sign and secure before Christmas so we could just enjoy the season. It wasn't really a word from God, it was my own desire that I wanted to for us and I held it over the process that God was taking us on.

Before Christmas, we had two options that we were really looking at. One was a big beautiful house with pillars. Only forty minutes away from Paris, it was on the RER train line and could fit thirty people. So it was a good option especially since we didn't have many and it was affordable. We called it the Russian house because the owners were Russian.

The second place was a large apartment with about ten bedrooms and was on the metro line, closer into the city. We called it the Snake House because this apartment had hallways that moved in and out like a snake. It was also affordable, but would be squishy putting thirty people in there. As we were processing with the two real estate agents for these houses, they were not saying no to us. So this was already a big step.

We did finally get our first yes with the Russian House and that was a big celebration as we had for months been getting no after no after no for renting. So after we got the yes for the Russian House, Adam and I brought three of our staff members to come see it and pray over this option. We looked it over and met the owner, the house was beautiful and had an amazing yard and could work, but it just didn't seem fully right.

It was far from the city and hard to get around but we kept moving forward with it. After that meeting they said to come back in a few days and sign the papers and it would all be official. This was a few days before Christmas. It seemed to be working out. We knew this house wasn't going to be forever. It was a stepping stone to then trust for another place closer to Paris.

The day came for us to sign the papers. I woke up with a bad feeling. Something felt off and wrong.

I told Adam we cannot rent this place. Adam was surprised and wasn't sure what else we could do. It's Christmas in a few days and in under two weeks we have to move and we have students arriving for a DTS and we have no place to go. It was true. But I just knew it wasn't right. We couldn't do it. Adam agreed he felt off as well. So we called one of our elders in Australia, Cliff Wrener for help.

Cliff had the key for us and he said, "If one or either of you feel off about this, absolutely do not sign those papers and don't get the house."

That sat so well with us and as we prayed we felt God say not to do it.

We decided we were not getting the Russian House. It looked good on paper and it fit us and it was our first yes, but we knew we couldn't, something was off about it and we didn't want to risk it, even if we didn't fully understand.

So we called the real estate agent and had to tell them that we would not rent the property. It was not an easy call to make. It was a Friday December 22nd. Adam and I were driving and we realized we were back to square one. No Russian House. The Snake House was not getting back to us and we learned that in France, if they don't get back to you even when you leave a lot of messages, that means it's a no. They just don't want to tell you directly. So, no Snake House either.

Later that same afternoon, everyone was on holidays now so we couldn't see any more houses and we couldn't get a hold of anyone. We needed to move out of Bois-Colombes latest on January 4th and we had students starting to arrive January 3rd through 6th. The DTS started January 7th. We didn't know what we were going to do.

Christmas happened and it was all you could ask for in a Christmas. Lots of fun, food, family time and presents. A staff member's supporter sent us money for a big turkey. Another staff's parent gave us money for decorations and food to make it more special. So we went all out. We had abundance of food and presents and decor! It was amazing. A Christmas that many of us will never forget. We gave glory to God and took four days to rest and have fun together.

The whole time though, in the back of my mind, I was worried.

Each day was a countdown of what was to come. I struggle with high responsibility which at times leads to worry which isn't good as worry is not from God! It's clear in scripture in Matthew 6 - Do not worry! But I would play off my responsibility as being just that. Actually though, it was a lack of trust and faith in God and what He can do.

Yes, I was leading this base, and yes, I was leading the DTS that was coming up and responsible for their lives and that they would have a home to live in. But ultimately, God told me to move to Paris and start this base. So actually it's His problem, and not mine. I just need to be faithful with the little He has called me to do and He will do the rest.

I will do the possible, and I need to trust Him to do the impossible!

December 27 rolled around. It was time to start seeing more buildings. It was one week away from our moving deadline of January 4th.

We also had advice from on our leaders to have a backup option ready. So online we found a big old farm house two hours north of Paris and literally in the middle of nowhere. Just fields all around it. No houses for miles. It was a direct rental through the owner. He had said yes we can rent it for three months. Come and sign the papers on Saturday.

So we talked it over with our staff team and showed them picture of the building. It wasn't pretty, but it was big. It was in an area called Chars. We had until Saturday morning, only three days, to find something else or we were signing this house for three months. We would have to live in Chars.

Our staff took it well and we went into a time of worship. During that worship time we started praying out loud. A lot of us cried and said to God that we would lay down our rights, and we would go wherever He wanted us to go. Even if it's Chars, we will go to Chars.

I cried and prayed the same prayer. After months of trusting for a place in or near the city and getting all these words about Paris, I was making sure my heart was right and willing to go to Chars for three months until we could find something else.

It was deep for all of us, personally and corporately. We laid down our expectations and dreams of what the New Year would look like and adjusted to the reality of what could be happening. God was faithful. His words were still true. So we committed afresh to him to however he wanted to lead us we would do it.

The next day was Thursday the 28th. The whole day we looked and still found nothing.

I went to my room that night around 8pm by myself and prayed, "God, come on please. I'm willing to go to Chars, but I really really don't want to and it will be so hard to run a DTS in the middle of nowhere. Especially when the students are told it's run in Paris! I don't want to deceive them. God please open a door."

I then started researching on Airbnb and looked at houses that had at least five bedrooms. I felt we could work with five bedrooms. We could squish some bunk beds in there and move some things around. I found only one house that was just to the east of the city in a suburb called Pantin. The house was 750 sq. meters (8072 square feet). So it was a good size and it said the house could host twelve people. But for that amount of space I knew it could host at least thirty YWAMers. So I did a last ditch effort and wrote the owner and message.

I shared we were a non-profit organisation and needed a place for three months and asked if we could rent it.

He got back to me with a quick, "Yes."

Amazing! I then asked, "Can we host twenty to thirty people in the house?"

To my surprise, he replied with another, "Yes."

Feeling the exciting momentum, I then wrote him and asked him for a renting price, but he wasn't responding. So I closed my laptop and fell asleep.

The morning of Friday, December 29th arrived. Six days until we needed to move. After we finished worship together as a base, I checked my messages: the Airbnb house owner had given us his phone number. Adam and I started communicating with him and he gave us a large amount to rent the house for three months, way over what we could afford. But we had nothing to lose so we asked him one more impossible question.

"Can we rent it for 1/3 of the price that you're asking for?"

To our amazement, he responded with a, "Yes!"

He wasn't back in Paris until Sunday to show us the house. But we were able to go look at it because his cleaners could open the house for us at noon. So Adam and I jumped in our car and drove to the east of the city to see the house.

Could this be it? I thought, *Could this be the answer to prayer we have been trusting and waiting months for?*

When we arrived at the house it looked like a big white wall with big grey garage doors. It seemed nice and secure which I like. But there was nothing special or significant looking at the outside of the building and I wondered, *How is there going to be a big enough house behind this wall for us to fit thirty people?*

The street the house was on was a low income area. You could tell by the garbage on the street and the high rise buildings, which easily had multiple families crammed into it. We were in a typical french neighborhood, but it was more like an actual "hood". I took comfort from the big garage doors that were almost twice my height because one of my biggest prayers was that we would have a home, a base, that was safe for our students and staff.

We met the cleaners, who didn't speak French but English as they were from Hong Kong, and came over with the owner when he moved. We found out he works for a bank and owns a house in Hong Kong and in Paris which was this house and also had an apartment in the city.

We stepped into the house. It has a long beautiful hallway that goes the whole length of the building. As you walk down stairs separate the hallway you have to the right a staircase that goes up and a staircase going down. As you continue the hallway, it leads into the open floor plan of a kitchen on your right and to the left a pair of giant sliding glass doors that shape around the outdoor courtyard.

The main room was a big L shape with another set of glass sliding doors all around it. The kitchen was to the right of the L shape and it opened into a large room with so much natural light. It had the main meeting room with a high ceiling and a grand piano and it also had three separate rooms, divided by walls, that broke up the main room into two more lounge spaces.

It was a big space and could easily host thirty to forty people comfortably for hanging out and worship times. Above the large room was a huge loft bedroom with a big bathroom, a walk-in closet, and space for ten girls with bunk beds. The house was big and the layout was nice for common space. But the bedrooms would be unique to squish people into.

We looked all around and liked it, but I remember leaving still feeling a bit unknown with how we could make the space all happen!

We returned home. Now, we had to make a decision about canceling the meeting the next morning with the owner in Chars and then committing to this owner and this Airbnb rental in Pantin. It was time to pray.

Pantin is a neat suburb in the East. It is on the metro line and still very much a part of the city with shops and people everywhere. It would be easy for us as a base to get in and out of Paris and easy to explore and do all the things God was calling us to do.

We felt to say no to Chars. So we called the owner to cancel our meeting the next day. For me, this was still a huge risk. The

Pantin house owner had only given us his verbal word of confirmation.

We arranged to meet the owner of the Pantin house on the Sunday night to sign the papers and give a deposit. We met with the owner with much still undecided. When we met him we asked, "Could we move in on Monday, January 1st?"

"Yes" was his reply, which now seemed like the normal answer for us.

So we asked another question, "Could we put in bunk beds and move the furniture around?"

Again he said, "Yes."

We felt God say it was right and we signed the papers and took the keys and quickly drove home to tell our staff that we were moving in on the first of January! As we got home we then pulled everyone together and told them and showed them pictures of our new home! They were ecstatic! It was a mansion and it was beautiful and it was not two hours away in Chars! They were all so so excited! We gave honour and glory to God for his provision. And prayed blessings over the owner for being so generous with us.

The next night God told Adam and I to get away to a hotel for a night. It had been such a stressful season for us. We had been learning to trust God in so many ways.

So we went to a nice hotel with a pool and relaxed. I was amazed as we got to the hotel and went into the pool how quickly stress started to leave my body. I was stressed. We were stressed and overwhelmed. I just lay in the water in a bubble massage area and started to fall asleep lying there and allowing the last few weeks or worry and unknowns just go.

Peace started to come back and relief began to come.

As I lay there, a water aerobics class began on the other side of the pool. With pool noodles under his arms and surrounded by little old ladies, Adam joined in. He was happy and relaxing as he did his hour aerobics. I relaxed as I just lay there amazed at what was happening with our new little base. The night was wonderful.

We went out for Chinese food and had nice time being husband and wife and not just base leaders.

We woke up, had breakfast and had to get back to the base by 10am, as we needed to pack and clean the house. We were rested, but still in the midst of the battle to move and get into the New Year.

It was December 31 and the relief for Adam and I was massive especially after signing the papers and getting the keys. We met the owner in the afternoon of the 31st and he was nice and genuinely desired to help and knew the house could be used for something good as he wasn't using it.

We signed the papers and it was all official. The house was ours for three months.

We drove away after meeting with him with the keys and papers in our hands feeling so excited and so thrilled for what God was doing. We went back home and walked into the house to find our staff busily cleaning and packing their bags. The new keys dangling in our hands, we all celebrated! It was 100% official now! We were moving the next morning!

We finished cleaning and packing as much as we could, and then we told our staff to enjoy the New Year. Many went downtown Paris to the Champs-Élysées to see the fireworks and welcome in the New Year that way. Adam and I and a few of us stayed home and relaxed.

Just before midnight Adam and I jumped on the scooter and drove to La Grande Arche which is in La Defense. La Grande Arche, which means the big arch, is aligned on the same road as the Arc de Triomphe. So both Arches face each other. La Grande Arche is massive compared to the Arc de Triomphe but as you sit on the steps of La Grande Arche you can see the Arc de Triomphe in the distance.

The fireworks were being let off from the Arc de Triomphe and so Adam and I thought we would watch them from a distance on the steps. We arrived and there was a group of people with the same idea. We all sat together looking towards the little arch quietly in the cold waiting for the New Year to roll around.

It was a surreal moment once again, realizing where we were. Myself being from the West Coast of Canada from Vancouver Island, I grew up on a hobby farm and went to a Christian school. I had been through my parents' divorce and other family pains.

Who am I to be sitting here in Paris counting down the New Year and leading a pioneering work with my handsome New Zealander husband? What is my life? Never would I have dreamed to be doing this.

As I was reflecting and thinking of all of this, I never aspired to these things they just came about as I listen to that lovely still small voice. I wasn't anyone special, I just wanted to see people know God and know His deep love for them and the world. God changed my life and I wanted to give me life so other could be changed through Him.

The fireworks went off and it was midnight. 2018 was upon us.

We sat there for a moment more, kissed as was custom for welcoming in the New Year, then stood up and left. We got back on our scooter and drove home, ready to welcome in January.

So many unknowns ahead. Our first DTS as YWAM Paris Central. New staff were arriving and a new house. So much to take on. But we went to bed happy to know that yes there were a lot of things to take care of, but at least we all have a roof over our heads for the next three months.

JANUARY

"For no matter how many promises God has made, they are 'Yes' in Christ. And so through him the 'Amen' is spoken by us to the glory of God."

2 Corinthians 1:20 (NIV)

January was suddenly here. I was still dealing with the stress and pressure of the previous month's house hunt. Everything was so surreal as we moved into a new place and worked to set up a home. On one hand, it was easy to adjust because I was so use to the transient missionary life, but it was also very hard to process how fast it all happened. My joy and relief of having a property caused my worries to die down and focus now to set up a home for our new incoming school and staff.

The house seemed like an old warehouse that was converted into a modern hipster style home. It was large. Over 750 square meters of living space. The common areas were not a problem for us. It was the bedrooms. We had permission to put thirty people in this house. Except that, we were going to need another place.

Because in a few days as students came and then soon more staff would come we would be well over thirty five people!

As we examined the five bedrooms (yes only five!), we calculated how many bunk beds and mattresses we could put in each room. With some much experience in YWAM, I can now gage a room by how many bunk beds I can fit into it. I'm quite confident in this art. Adam and I have had long discussions on how many imaginary bunks could fit in rooms—enjoyably I might add. So we came to our conclusions on bunks and positioning.

We now needed more than double the amount of beds. And we needed actually physical bunk beds! Also, we didn't have tables or chairs or linens. For this need we called our friends in YWAM Biarritz. Before we left, they had said that once we found a place to let them know and they would give us mattresses, bunk beds, tables, and chairs.

So we told them we found a place and the next day they rented a truck and filled it full and drove it up to Paris for us! It was perfect numbers and perfect timing! We had no money to buy any of those items and it was incredible to see God's perfect provision for us once again! The adventure with getting all the donations and items was setting it all up in time and preparing the rooms before the students started arriving!

Like good YWAMers, we took to building bunks beds, moving furniture, and arranging rooms. We made a bedroom in the basement for the staff and student boys. It had no windows or a lot of space, but we made it has homey as we could. The top loft bedroom we were able to squeeze eleven girls and mattresses scattered along the ground in a somewhat nice fashion, but when actual bodies and suitcases arrived it became a lot more chaotic and squishy. Yet, all the girls handled it with gratitude and no complaining.

Another room we lined up three bunk beds in for our staff and student girls. The room also had a loft with a completely vertical ladder that we shoved four other mattresses up with four of our staff girls. Again, all were happy and content because our biggest victory was at least having a home to go to. I think the gratitude naturally poured over into the students as they arrived, because we shared with them the story and about God's provision.

Adam and I took a room and another room went to our guest speakers that would come each week to speak on the DTS. The last room went to a married couple that was on the DTS.

After this we knew we still needed space. We had another couple on the DTS that we need to give a room to and we had more new staff arriving and had no more space to put them! So I started searching on Airbnb again.

Quickly I found a three bedroom quirky looking house that was a thirty minute walk away. It was a good price and meant we could fill it up with more people as we went along. So Adam and I prayed together, knowing it would mean more finances and more commitment but knowing we needed it.

God said yes, go for it and trust Him - He's got this.

We quickly clicked the reserve button on the house and started moving in four of our staff the next day and got another room ready for the DTS couple that was arriving that weekend.

God told me that as a base we would grow quickly and establish quickly and that we needed to move on His momentum.

We experienced that quickly especially since a week before we had twelve people with a two month house rental and now we're over thirty five people with two different houses with three month rentals within the first week of January! Things were moving quickly and God was moving us at this pace.

We were able to get the bunk beds up and move the house around to fit the number we needed to. Everyone got a bed and a space, even if it was squishy we made it work and we celebrated the small things. The students started arriving one by one within a span of five days. Our numbers doubled in size and the house was filled with noise, laughter and conversations as people began getting to know each other well.

The first two days of the school started wonderfully! We had orientation about who we were and about YWAM France and YWAM International. We had a registration day for the DTS and had all the students' photos taken and to give them all information about what the next six months would look like. I felt we were doing pretty good and felt we looked good as a base. Which was important to me because only one week earlier I was freaking out about having no accommodation for this school!

The kitchen crew was also doing an incredible job, cooking lunch and dinner every day and going from twelve people to thirty five people. Adam and I received the value of community and family, and eating meals together twice a day, from being on staff at YWAM Perth for so many years.

Yes, it is easier to do buffet style and yes it is easier to not do meals all together, but the value of having a family style meal daily for us shows care and belonging to everyone who comes. It creates a healthy community.

So we knew with starting a base that our emphasis was the same, family and valuing everyone and meals twice a day together. The first week of the DTS started on a Wednesday, and the students learned about "Hearing God's Voice & Quiet Times." We had our good friends from Biarritz, Timo & Grace Kraft, come for the week. Grace spoke on the topic beautifully.

After the first morning of teaching something started changing.... We had one student already not doing well but I thought, *Ok, it's just one student it should be ok.*

After dinner things really started not going well... One of our staff started throwing up and then I walked into the kitchen and one of our students started throwing up in the sink and then one by one 30 out of the 35 people had violent diarrhea and vomiting for hours!

We tucked people in and cleaned up a lot of throw up and said goodnight to everyone and encouraged people to get some sleep. All throughout the night I lay in my bed hearing constant sound of sickness and noises that were very unpleasant. I got up at one point in the dark and was ready to go down and help or something.

God said, "Go back to bed Leah, there's nothing you can do. It's ok." So I lay back down and tried to get some sleep. Around 5:30am I woke up and went downstairs to survey our newly set up base.

It was like a war zone. I've never seen anything like it!

There were bodies throughout the hallways on the floors... buckets and garbage cans were around the various heads and just general sickness and mess was everywhere. I wasn't sure where to start or what to do. I went back upstairs to my lovely sleeping husband, who didn't wake up once in the night, and woke him up.

"I need help." I said. He looked at me a bit confused.

"What do you need help with?"

"Oh...I don't know...I just need...need support."

"Ok." He smiled. So he came down stairs and immediately was in the game. He went out bought cleaning supplies. He cleaned up the bodies and helped put them on couches and in beds and the base started looking like a base again. We had class again that morning and ended up having only five people—the rest were sleeping. The morning after, everyone was recovering from what we still refer to this day, as the "green plague."

To make the tension of that week worse, the owner's wife showed up in the middle of our little fiasco unannounced. Now she was not the approving kind. She was polite but harsh in her dealings with perfectionism and control. It became a tension throughout our three months at the house to meet a standard that was never possible to meet, especially with thirty people living within the house. We soon had to make boundaries with her saying she can't just show up unannounced and come in, which was respected.

So from then on she told us when she was arriving and we made the house as perfect as we could and sent everyone out of the house when she came. It worked well, but every time she came there was always something wrong with what we did.

As a community we started praying for her and her husband. Praying for them to know God and be at peace. We prayed also for blessings to come over them as they blessed us by letting us stay there that they would see a hundredfold blessing on themselves. We still pray even though the relationship ended in tension. We believe we did our utmost to love and take care of their house the best we could.

After the green plague and a deep level of bonding that you can only get when everyone shares how much bodily fluids they lost from either end, our schedule continued. We went into the following weeks with ease as we came together for worship and intercession times.

The DTS continued to learn week by week on the various subjects of Nature & Character of God, Repentance and Forgiveness and Worship and Intercession. More depth came into the school and into the base as our eyes continually focused on God and soon our morning hallways were not littered with bodies with sickness, but people in various corners of the house having close and intimate times with God.

People are hungry to know God deeper and learn His ways. It's beautiful seeing that even in the mess of not having it all organized well, and not having the perfect DTS booklet or living situation, that people still just wanted to seek God.

In YWAM we can get hung up on structure and order—which are good things. But ultimately in a DTS, people come because they want to meet with God—to discover His voice on a deeper level and have a time of discipleship. It happened quickly and it was gorgeous. Seeing nineteen hungry hearts wanting to go deeper and wanting to understand.

I sat in Repentance and Forgiveness on week three thinking, *I love what I do. Yes, it's hard and tiring at times, but I wouldn't trade this...It is so worth it.* Seeing people grow in understanding of their personal walk with God is something I can't compare to anything else.

In my younger years, before YWAM, I dreamed about what I wanted to do with my life. Besides my unrealistic dream of being an actor, I dreamt of owning my own summer camp. I loved summer camp. You get to live together and have fun together and learn cool things together. That was my biggest dream.

God took that dream and made it not just for the summer but for my life. I literally live a summer camp style living every day with community, young people, teaching, and growth. Even better, I get to do it in Paris of all places!

I am amazed at God's care in the details. He knows me and knows how I work and what gives me life and purpose. It's incredible living the dream with Jesus. He took my little nice dream and blew it out of the water. From running my own summer camp to leading a YWAM base in one of the most beautiful cities in the world.

FEBRUARY

"Truly I tell you," Jesus replied, "no one who has left home or brothers or sisters or mother or father or children or fields for me and the gospel will fail to receive a hundred times as much in this present age..."

Mark 10:29-30 (NIV)

Week five's topic of the DTS was Relationships with my good friend from Perth, Amy Garis teaching. She is a beautiful woman with great joy and perspective on how to live life well with others and with Jesus. I really love her and love the insight she brings to me and the people around her!

Relationships week is always a big week. It brings up pains and hurts from the past. It shows when relationships were done wrong and not in line with the standards of God. It brings a healthy confrontation to where we need to raise the standard on how to live well according to the first and second commandment.

This week was even more confronting to me because my precious little brother arrived in Paris to visit me for a few weeks.

He was struggling at home with life and school, and he needed a change. So my mom asked him if he wanted to visit his big sister and brother-in-law in Paris. Of course he said sure!

I have always have had such a soft spot for my brother. I am fourteen years older than him and had been in missions for the majority of his life. I wasn't there to watch him grow up, which was one of my biggest sacrifices with responding to being in missions. Leaving my family, but specifically leaving Levi, and trusting him into God's care. So having him come was wonderful and then on relationships week as well!

So I thought, he's seventeen and could benefit from the teaching, *So why not join the DTS in lectures with me for the next few weeks while he is with us?*

He joined classes and the students accepted him in as a friend right away. It worked so well. During his first class time, we had a time of praying out and Levi prayed out loud. I was so shocked and impressed at his quickness to respond and receive the teaching. That week went by well. He learned and started making friends with the school and people on base.

The next week of lectures was Lordship with Mark Parker. Lordship is about making Jesus the Lord of your life. It means a full surrender to living out Jesus's words "Take up your cross and follow me." So this was already a big week and Mark was an amazing passionate speaker that truly challenges people to the core. This made me think, *Well if Levi is here why not have him jump in head first into this teaching and see what happens.*

Monday morning came. And we started by listening to a song to get the class ready and pumped for the week. This is Mark's teaching style. I love how Mark teaches as it forces people to get out of their comfort zone. Especially in our day and age as people long to be comfortable. So if Mark, an older ywamer, can jump around the classroom then us youngins can as well.

Mark grabbed his old-school ipod, went through the thousands of songs and picked a song from the movie, *The Greatest Showman,* "From Now On." The lyrics of the song were projected on the wall. We all started reading and singing the song. The song starts off slow and I remember thinking, *Wow, these lyrics are very powerful.*

As the song continued, it got faster and a chorus erupted loudly with, "...and we will come back home and we will come back home again!" We all caught on quickly and felt the power of the song and the presence of God fill the room. We were not just singing any song; we were singing about coming home to Jesus. To not be blinded by the ways of the world, but to see clearly and return closely to our saviour. Emotions filled the room. We were connecting with our God. The song ended. Silence filled the room as we processed what just happened.

Mark walked back and forth at the front of the class. He then pointed at Levi and asked,

"Levi, what is happening with you?" Levi was standing directly behind me. Unsure of what was happening and didn't want to turn around to be the overbearing sister, I stood and waited.

Levi responded, "Umm… I'm not sure."

Mark asked, "What are you feeling; what is happening inside you?"

Levi then broke down in tears. He just started weeping. Mark came over and hugged him. I turned around. Levi collapsed in Mark's arms and wept even more. I then just broke down in awe of what was happening—*My little brother whom I have been praying for for years is having a deep healing moment of knowing the love of God.* I have never seen such softness and tenderness like this in Levi.

A lot of people in the classroom started crying. Mark affirmed Levi and then finished hugging Levi. We then just all sat down, wiped our faces, and class continued.

From that moment Levi became a sponge to the teaching: ready to listen, ready to learn. He came to me a few days after that moment with Mark and said he wanted to stay, to complete the DTS. I started thinking logically about him finishing high school and about him needing a visa and tickets and finances etc. But Levi knew what he wanted and didn't want to stop what the Lord was doing in his life.

On Friday of the Lordship week we have application where we apply everything we have learned in the week. During application, Levi had a time of repentance and forgiveness and then fully surrendered his life to God and got baptized. It was such a powerful moment of transformation and change and commitment to Christ.

During this week, I also had a huge revelation from my own life. In 2004 in Perth, Australia where I did my DTS we had Mark Parker speaking on Lordship and during application for me my biggest surrender was Levi. I never could have imagined fourteen years later I would be leading a base in Paris, have Mark speaking on my school, and the same little brother I surrendered to God be with me and get fully saved on the same week. God's faithfulness to me and my family just blew me away.

I was amazed again at the scripture, *"Truly I tell you,"* said *Jesus, no one who has left home or brothers or sisters or mother or father or children or fields for My sake and for the gospel will fail to receive a hundredfold in the present age—houses and brothers and sisters and mothers and children and fields..."* (Mark 10:29 NIV).

Often we think we are the ones that have to bring the change and be there for the change in our family, but through our obedience God takes care of them and protects them. I see that clearer than ever now.

As I started processing Levi staying, the weeks carried on beautifully. Next week we had was Father Heart of God with my good friend Cliff Wrener. He and his wife, Cristine, have been great friends and mentors to me and Adam for years. They were huge influencers to us and people we deeply cherished. Every year I'd try to have them teach on my DTS's as there was such an anointing in what they brought! Father Heart of God week was healing and restoring for the DTS, many people getting healed of wounds and started to see God rightly.

Levi never had a father. I watched as a deep love infused into Levi from Father God. God's hand was just all over him and Levi was transformed by it as well as the rest of the school. Such a special week for all of us.

Another crazy thing with Levi staying was having to figure out outreach for him. It was a Backpack Europe DTS so all of the students that come get six month visas to stay in Europe. Levi came into Europe on a visitor's visa which allowed him ninety days within the Schengen Area. I already had a sense of which team Levi was to join and he had the same sense, but I had to figure out days and numbers to make sure he had enough days. Some of the nations he was going to was out of the Schengen region like Dublin, Cyprus, and Albania so it gave him more time.

So I sat down and started counting the dates and days and locations. I counted how many days he would be in France with us and for a week back for report back at the end of the school and then the nations on outreach and when his flight was leaving back to Canada. As I added it up I was amazed that the number came to exactly ninety days! Which meant it was perfect on his visitor's visa in Europe!

God orchestrated Levi coming and staying down to every detail! Once again I am amazed at God's faithfulness and care over us and me and my family. Levi was excited. It all fell it to place so quickly.

Throughout this season Adam and I realized it was time to invite more people onto our leadership team. For the first couple months as a base, it was just Adam and I leading everything.

We would have "leaders meetings" at McDonald's or else we would just be sitting on our bed in our bedroom as we didn't have anywhere else to go. So, thank you Lord for McDonald's. Plus, that McDonald's was actually really nice. We would sit at the McCafe. I would order a rooibos vanilla tea with a muffin and Adam would order the four-euro kids meal, which was quite a deal with a cheeseburger, drink, fries and an ice cream! Even though those were good meetings, we knew it couldn't just be the two of us making decisions for all the running of the base and the running the DTS's as well. So we prayed and discussed what was best. Two people on our base stood out to us.

One was Thierry Noamessi. He was already standing out as a leader amongst us and was always willing to serve. Our other choice was Bethany Burnett. A gorgeous and anointed woman from Colorado. She was on staff with us in Biarritz as well and had been a part of our Music DTS's for the last four years because if her amazing talents in music! Bethany also had a great ability in seeing things from different angles than us, which was what we needed! Both Thierry and Bethany were gifted leaders and influencers so we were excited to ask them to pray about joining us. Within a few weeks, they both got back with a yes from God, and we formed our first leadership team.

Soon after they joined the battle continued for our fight for our next accommodation! February was ending and we were two months into our three month contract. We had to be out of this Airbnb by the end of March.

So God started speaking to us about three mountains that we needed to see moved. The first mountain was accommodation: finding a permanent place for us as a base. We didn't want to keep moving every three months and living out of our bags. So we felt to pray and fight for the mountain of accommodation to be moved and to see ourselves get established as YWAM Paris Central.

The second mountain was finances. As a base we still needed to buy a lot more items to be running as an organization and a base. We needed finances to for down payments on the accommodations we were looking at. If you rent a building, you have to usually put down two to three months' rent as a caution. So for us that meant needing at least €8,000 to put down on a place if we found it. We didn't have any finances as all our fees were being used for: food, accommodation, electricity, water bills, car, and gas and more..

The third mountain, was trying to get more students for the upcoming April Music DTS. It was just about a month away. We had one student accepted and none pending. Usually at a month before a school starts we would have all the students accepted and just be gathering arrival details and answering packing questions. So we felt we had to pray and fight for more students to come and see this mountain moved. We started praying for these mountains be moved before us.

MARCH

"See! The winter is past; the rains are over and gone.

Flowers appear on the earth; the season of singing has come, the

cooing of doves is heard in our land."

Song of Songs 2:11-12 (NIV)

With three mountains to see moved before the end of March, it became more of a reality of how much needed to happen in four weeks. The Backpack Europe DTS was going on outreach in three weeks. We had to clean, reorganize the house, and move to our new location. The pace quickened.

We felt God was leading us every worship and intercession time to keep fighting for these mountains to be moved. It was incredible to see the whole base and the DTS get behind this fight. We were all in it together.

The scripture that stood out the most was Matthew 17:20, *"Truly I tell you, if you have faith as small as a mustard seed, you can say to this mountain, 'Move from here to there,' and it will move. Nothing will be impossible for you."* (NIV)

So we approached the throne room of God with boldness! Asking our God and Father for impossible things. We prayed and asked for names for people for the DTS and had times of waiting on the Lord to ask people we knew back at home if they wanted to come to the DTS. Responses started to come back. Applications came in.

We even met a family visiting from Germany that had an Airbnb near us. They knew of YWAM and wanted to get to know us as a base. They joined us for worship times and prayer times and we just fell in love with their kids. They had two little ones. They were just precious to our community. The couple, Martin and Leah, and their two little ones, Anna and Daniel, soon became good friends to Adam and I. It was so nice for us to have another married couple around!

They invited Adam and I to their place for a meal. During our evening together, I was sitting there feeling so refreshed as Adam and I hadn't been out with another married couple in a while!

It was a breath of fresh air for sure to make new friends that were around our age and who we connected with quite well.

I suggested to Adam that they should do the Music DTS. Adam didn't think they would have time for that. Martin was in Paris for three months doing his PHD and Leah was taking care of the kids. But sure enough soon the conversation came up and Martin asked Adam about the details. God lined it up so well and they ended up applying for the DTS!

A true miracle, the Music DTS went from one student to nine students in three weeks! Other people had friends at home they invited to come and those friends felt to come! God was faithfully leading the School the way it was meant to go. We were seeing the mountain of student numbers being moved!

The next mountain, we saw moved was the one of finances. As a pioneering base we were still living month by month for our accommodation and needs. We needed finances in two areas—the rental deposit for our next property in April and outreach fees. For the DTS outreach, we needed around €14,000.

The day before the finances were due for the students and their outreach we still needed all of it. That morning in lectures we learned about Spiritual Authority. We had a time of prayer and asked God what we could do in regards to the finances. As we waited on the Lord some people felt to give financially. Other students felt to have a prayer time in the afternoon and not to stop praying until they saw all the finances come in.

So that afternoon the students set up a white board and wrote the amount they needed and put a bowl underneath the sign. They started praying. Soon the bowl started filling with money! The number on the whiteboard starting going down and down.

I was having meetings in the afternoon and was hearing different moments of screaming and rejoicing as the afternoon went by. They kept praying and having worship together and different staff and students were writing people at home and calling people to see the finances come in. The number on the whiteboard kept going down. They kept seeing finances come. The faith in the group started growing and growing!

One of the students had a word that all the finances would come in by dinner time. I finished my meetings and came to join the school; it was around 6pm and dinner is at 6:30pm. We all gathered in the main room and pretty much the whole base was involved. We started praying and worshiping and trusting to see all the finances come in before dinner! I looked at the whiteboard and saw that the school only needed around €1000 left! It was incredible! God was providing and the mountain was being moved!

We kept praying and the number went down to €500 and then someone else say they wanted to give and the number went down some more and then finally one last person shouted out from the group, "I'll pay off the rest!!"

We all screamed in excitement and started dancing around the room!

Adam ran to the sound board and cranked on the song, "Days of Elijah." We sang and danced and gave thanks to God for his incredible provision. It was like in Exodus 15 after the Red Sea crossing, Moses and Miriam sang a song in celebration and thanksgiving to God. We all were singing and giving God praise. At the bridge of the song we got even louder singing,

"There's no God like Jehovah. There's no God like Jehovah."

It was such an amazing moment. The song finished. We excitedly gathered around the tables and had a wonderful meal all together. Everyone received the finances they needed to go on outreach and be a blessing to the nations.

Our faith was all soaring! God was moving the mountain of finances and releasing to us all that the school needed. It was a celebration and testimony to these students that God was for them and not against them---that he was with them and he was a God who provides! This was a story that would carry so many of them and a moment of reminder that God moves on our behalf.

So we danced and sang and gave honour and glory to God and then sat down and had a wonderful joyous dinner all together! God was moving and they were ready for outreach. They were leaving for outreach in two weeks. Now tickets could be bought and preparations made.

The other part of the financial mountain was housing. No matter what accommodation came our way the landlords always asked for at least a two month deposit. We had no savings as a base. We were literally living month by month with our rentals and expenses. So we needed to somehow have at least €8,000 for a down payment. It was a halfway through March. We knew the whole time this was what we needed and not sure where it was coming from.

One day out of the blue and unexpected, someone gave us €9,000. It was extraordinary. We hadn't had time to ask around or send out requests. It was God's miraculous hand upon us and some amazing generous people. I was so amazed and encouraged again at God's provision. We met as a leadership team and all of us were just in awe. The second mountain was moving. We had the ability to put a deposit on a house.

The problem was we had no house to put that deposit on. It was the middle of March and we needed to move out by March

31st. We needed to move to a new place and set up for the Music DTS before April 8th.

Adam and Thierry had done a great job searching for places. I lead the DTS classes in the mornings and spent the afternoons out with Adam looking at rentals and meeting owners.

Nothing was working.

However, this time the approach was way different. I wasn't as worried. I learned my lesson in faith and trust with getting this last house…or I didn't have time to be worried. There was peace knowing that God was already doing so much in our midst. He was going to make away again. My prayer was more about wanting to have longer than just a three month rental. It was wearing on us. We were all still living out of little bags and wanted to have a home to unpack and be there for a while. So we kept searching.

Adam wanted to stop looking at houses and start looking at renting a warehouse that we could develop into a base. I was skeptical but really up for anything as we had no options before us. From our days in Perth, we learned we could develop a warehouse into a great base of operations. The old base there was a massive warehouse that they had converted into a base with a huge dining room and a worship area that could hold over five hundred people. So the search was on.

Soon Adam found a promising option that was for rent from the owner. We had learned over time that real estate agents don't trust associations. So we felt to only approach owners because we needed the direct communication and contact to explain we were legit people and honourable renters.

We travelled to this warehouse in the north of Paris in suburb called Aubervilliers. The owner took us in and rolled up the big warehouse door and it was an empty shell of a warehouse. My idea of a home for my staff and students were images of a warm fireplace and room to run around and be comfortable in…This was a big room with high ceilings, no insolation, bare walls, and concrete floors. It was cold. I was not overly pleased.

The owner took us upstairs to the apartment above the warehouse. It had a warm feel with four bedrooms, an open living space with potential for a kitchenette and living room. Adam and I made imaginary bunk bed calculations and determined it could hold eighteen to twenty people. The downstairs warehouse had other rooms were we could fit more people. So that was better than nothing.

We told the owner we would need to install a kitchen and put 30 people in it. The owner was fine with that. He was positive and friendly and liked us! I'm not sure why, but he did. Adam absolutely loved it. To me, it had potential...maybe.

We kept looking and searching. Everything else fell through.

The warehouse owner said we could sign the papers and move in April 1st. We prayed as a leadership team and took Thierry and Bethany to see the warehouse. They both felt positive about it. The kicker for me and for all of us was when we met with the owner.

We explained who we were and what we wanted to do with the space. He not only said yes, but that he would also fix it up before we moved in! He told us that he would get his workers to insulate the warehouse, put up walls, and paint. He also had them build a doorway and front wall, so it wouldn't be just the metal warehouse door, but an actual proper entrance instead. Even more, he said that he would also install a second shower for us as there was only one in one of the bathrooms.

We nodded along with this and were like "Uhh yes..Thank you..Ok...Yess...That's great, thank you." I was about to say, "We could help...." Adam motioned to me though and mouthed quietly "Don't say that," so I stopped. The owner finished and said he would get it all done for us. And at no cost. NO COST. He was going to install and do all of that FOR FREE.

We left that meeting overjoyed and amazed. The favour of God over us was massive. We signed the papers nine days before we moved in. God was right on time for us. We gave our €8000 deposit and celebrated as a base again of God's faithfulness.

The DTS's final lecture week was on Fear of the Lord. I was teaching and also my mom came to visit! She wanted to see Levi before he headed out on outreach and it was so wonderful for me because she has never visited me in France before! It was amazing and such a blessing to finish the season at the Pantin house and to show my mom everything that God had done.

The Wednesday night of that week we had a commissioning for the January Backpack Europe DTS. We all dressed up and ate good food and prayed over the three teams going out! One team was heading to Dublin, Copenhagen, Albania, Lesvos, and Cyprus over the three months. Another team was heading to Sweden, Finland, Latvia, Bulgaria, and Lesvos. The final team went to Romania, Ukraine, Lesvos, Portugal, and Spain. It was a Backpack Europe DTS.

We tailored their outreach to be adventurous and also one of impact in the various locations. They were all set and we commissioned them into all God had for them. We prayed expectation over them to be led by God and to follow Him for the three months. And to expect God to move in powerful ways everywhere they went! We challenged them in the great commission and to tell everyone about Jesus and to serve any chance they got.

The next day they said their goodbyes, and each team headed out on their three month outreach adventure with Jesus! I loved this school. It was a joy to lead them and to send them out. I had put two leaders per team and was confident in their ability to lead and to hear God in the teams. So off they went.

We had one week to put the Pantin House back in order. We believe in the principle to leave a place better than the way you found it. That was our aim. The biggest task was packing up all of our large items and storing them until we had the moving truck. We piled up our bunk beds and extra mattresses, because had to move beds back to their original rooms and set that up again. Then we had to do a lot of deep cleaning on top of that!

Each evening that week after large days of cleaning and organizing we watch The Matrix series and the old Lara Croft movies. We had fun and bonded well a staff team as we were moving into a new and exciting season of a permanent home and a new DTS.

The moving truck came. We had to do four different loads to our new base. We had a lot of stuff! Two giant loads came from the Pantin house filled with chairs and tables and base items and bunk beds and lots of people's personal things. Then we had two more loads that we had to do from our storage unit!

We had the storage unit for six months and it was full of furniture, people's bags and items so we had to unload that in the same time. It was a busy couples days and soon the base was filled with an enormous pile...that we then were able to sort through and slowly make our base a home. It was liberating to have our own space and make our home a home. All of us were ready for stability in location and not needing to live with limited supplies. It was time to create a home and a full functioning YWAM base.

APRIL

"The Lord is my shepherd I shall not be in want...he restores my

soul."

Psalm 23:1 (NIV)

Aubervilliers was a suburb just north of Paris. The metro line seven ran right to where we lived and, at the time, there were construction plans for a metro line twelve to be a five minute walk from our door. So location wise, to the centre of Paris it was a great location.

Yet Aubervilliers wasn't your typical French suburb; it wasn't French at all really. Many different nations and cultures filled the area. Broken down homes, vacant buildings, and garbage lined the streets. There was little in the way of parks or vegetation. Walking down the street you would see African mommas with their matching outfits and beautiful colours. You'd see Muslim woman pushing their baby strollers. Then on the same street you'd see Jewish boys with their little yamakas. It was an interesting world to step into. A mixing pot of people and cultures. We were a group of thirty mostly white people. We stood out.

As we walked the streets, many eyes watched us. Often, men made comments. But we knew this was where God was calling us. The nations were at our doorstep.

One of our staff said, "If Jesus was to choose somewhere to live in Paris, I am sure he would choose Aubervilliers."

That struck me and stuck with me. Jesus wouldn't have lived in the nicest part of town. He would have gone to the place of need, and that was exactly where we were. There were a lot of broken people in Aubervilliers. Adam noticed how many people have physical ailments and illnesses. This was a place we could bring the love of God and share it on the streets.

We started setting up our base as we had one week until all the students started arriving for the Music DTS! It was a quick process moving from one house to another and then to set it up and make it home.

As soon as we moved into our base we knew again that we needed more living space. This place could only house thirty. We were growing bigger than that. And we needed a space for Martin and Leah and the kids. So I looked on a secondhand sales website called Leboncoin, and found a house that had four bedrooms and was only a seven minute walk from the base.

Adam and I met the owner and saw the house. The house wasn't anything special. When you walk through the gate you see a lot of white. White driveway, white walls on either side. A white house. It was an older house and well loved. The inside had a fresh coat of paint and as we walked in we saw a worker changing the electrics in the kitchen.

The owner told us that her family grew up in the house. We could tell there was sentimental value, and they didn't want to change too much to the house. It seemed nice enough, but the house was old and really could be torn down and rebuilt. But for us, we were happy with it. We could add to it and I knew our staff would make the most of it.

The owner said yes to us on the spot for renting! We were amazed at another yes for a three-year rental. So we put four of our long term staff in the house and Martin and Leah and their family! God provided again!

The DTS students arrived and started settling in. It was incredible to have nine students especially because weeks before we only had one. But we still felt that there could be more! A girl from Paris came to visit us who knew YWAM. After talking with us and meeting us, she told us God was speaking to her about doing the DTS. So she signed up and we then had ten students.

The faithfulness of God was overflowing. So we entered into the first week of the DTS excited and happy for all God was doing. Adam was leading the DTS so I was ready to set up our base and fight for the things we needed.

It was a beautiful warehouse with big tall ceilings and windows at the top. The owner did a great job with the installation and the fresh paint. But it was a shell and needed life and decor to make it more of a home instead of an institute. We also didn't have a kitchen.

The house in Pantin had a kitchen and sinks all built in, but for the warehouse there was nothing. So we had to buy a whole kitchen! Adam and I felt to not just get anything, but to invest in a stainless steel kitchen set so it lasts long and is moveable. So my daily routine was research and buying on Leboncoin for kitchen items and decor for the base!

Piece by piece we built our kitchen. I bought the items second-hand and tried to get good deals on all the other items we needed: a sink, an oven, a stove top, stainless steel benches, fridges and freezers. It took a lot of effort but was worth it in the end as it came together so beautifully! We had some items that didn't work so we sold them again on Leboncoin and then bought other items!

Adam and another staff installed exhaust fans. We put in a washing machine and dryer under the staircase. I also found an office building that was shutting down and was getting rid of office tables and bookcases. So we rented a truck and picked up tables, bookshelves and different pieces of furniture to make our base a functioning home. It was amazing and life soon took shape on our base and we kept rolling on in our schedule and function.

Now we had two different properties both with three year contracts, so things were looking good on our accommodation front. Adam and I were getting our own apartment that was in the same complex of the base. The owner had to redo the floors and walls. It was going to take a month to get it all done; so we stayed in the guest speaker room and another house until it was complete. Even with these accommodations, we could only host around thirty five to forty people. It wasn't enough for long term growth and development.

Also, summer was fast approaching, when we told the YWAM leaders of France we were starting a base in Paris they asked if we would take on the organisation and running of the Paris Je t'aime.

Paris Je t'aime was a two week evangelical outreach with teams coming from all around the world to join and be apart of reaching Paris for Jesus. The Paris Je t'aime outreach took a lot of organisation and also needing to accommodate and feed everyone coming to Paris. So it wasn't a small task to take on in our first year.

The national leader of France at the time, Denis Drugeau, had been running it for thirteen years. He knew it was time to pass it on. And with us being a new plant in Paris, he asked if we would run and organize it.

We said yes.

Now we were committed to host lots of people and run this event. It was a large task and numbers for the Paris Je t'aime were looking at getting to over a hundred people! The accommodation we had wouldn't be enough. I started searching for properties around Aubervilliers. There weren't a lot of options.

Although, one place in particular stood out to me that I kept going to. The listing said it was for offices. It was a three-storey peach coloured building with twelve rooms and a nice open courtyard. The price wasn't bad per month. It was something we could reach with the numbers that we were projecting to have for the summer. I showed Adam and told the leadership team.

We sat on it for a week. Then the last week of April on a Tuesday morning we arranged to see the property and meet the owner. We thought we might as well see it and see what we think. The peach house was a fifteen minute walk from our base and it was situated directly beside the metro.

That week was Repentance and Forgiveness on the Music DTS and one of our good friends and elders from YWAM Perth was speaking that week; Caleb Brownhill. Caleb's parents pioneered the YWAM work in Perth, Australia and that's where Adam and I did our DTS's and were staff for many years.

The YWAM work in Biarritz, France was a pioneered team from Perth led by Daniel & Kate Appa. Kate is Caleb's sister and daughter to Peter and Shirley Brownhill who continue to lead the work in Perth, Australia. We were very close with the Perth base and to the Brownhill family as they have been our inspiration and who we would look to often for wisdom and direction with pioneering a base in a large city.

It was significant for Caleb to be speaking on the DTS that week more than we realized. We invited him to come see the property with us on the Tuesday morning. We drove up to the house. It had tall gates that open and you can drive through, but there was a chain around the gates. We parked and went through a smaller single door.

As we walked into the court yard, it was quite spacious with overgrown trees and flower beds. To the right it had enough parking spots for at least six cars and to the right it wove around the side of the building with more space and flower beds. There were large walls from other properties that cornered in the courtyard but there were no windows in those buildings so it was secure and private.

We had a positive feeling walking into it. The owner greeted us. He was a nice man, soft spoken and didn't seem to pushy or trying to swindle us in any way. He led us through the building.

We walked into four different rooms on the ground floor with sinks in most of the rooms and two toilets. It used to be an old doctor's office. The first floor had another four rooms with two toilets rooms and the third floor had two smaller rooms and one giant room that could fit at least ten bunk beds (from what we predicted) and another toilet.

The potential of this property was massive! The space, the rooms, you could knock out a few walls and make more meeting space and lounges. Right now the building was built into a lot of rooms from it being a doctor's office. It just needed some love to change it around and make it a home. It even had a basement with another three rooms and a laundry room—so much more potential there as well! We were excited.

Most of these older buildings were cut up and made into apartments; they were not often all one piece. We talked to the owner about price and he came down a bit. So we said we would talk and pray and get back to him. We went back to the base and sat and processed for a minute with Caleb.

It was a lot for us to take on. We already had one big base, plus we were renting a second house. Now we were looking at renting another big property on top of that?

Only months earlier we were twelve people in a small house in the west of Paris—now we were looking at renting another place for three years with the potential to host over a hundred people in a few months! It was a risk.

We were still living month to month with our finances as a base, and we were still putting all the details together. We gathered together in room after we got back from looking at the property and started thinking through the implications and if we could financially afford it. Caleb was sitting with us but not saying anything, you could tell he was thinking.

Then Caleb turned to us and said, "I'm not sure if this is God or not but... why don't you guys run a July DTS?"

We turned to Caleb in shock. I started laughing.

This year was one of the most insane years of my life in terms of trusting God and being stretched for the impossible. We were already running three DTS's within our first fifteen months as a base and the thought of starting another DTS in two months sounded absurd and comical.

"Uhh, what?" I said.

"If you ran a July DTS then you could have more people and it could fit with getting a new building." Caleb explained. We all paused again. Surprisingly, it sat very well with me.

"It was on my mind to run an Unreached DTS to reach those who have never heard the gospel before." I eventually said. Adam was still processing the whole idea, but I started getting excited and coming around to it.

"That is a great idea," Caleb said. He was very supportive. We chatted a bit more and hummed and hawed over the idea, especially because July was only two months away and we would need a leader.

We took a few weeks to pray and process this as leaders… renting another larger building would mean another financial commitment as well. So as we prayed as leaders we felt like the building was a yes and we couldn't shake the idea that running a DTS in July was a yes as well.

We felt the building and the DTS were linked and we couldn't get one without the other!

So as we prayed and asked God if we should get the peach house we also prayed and ask if we should start a July DTS as well. The July DTS we felt should be focused on the unreached and we felt to call it the Frontline DTS that reaches to Asia, Middle East, and Africa.

As a leadership team, we all received a yes from God to move forward with the building and running the Frontline DTS. We had our yes from God, but it was still a risk as we needed the finances to have a deposit on the house and then we needed to get a new DTS ready in two months. We had no information online, no students or even potential students.

It was a lot of work and unknowns, but we have learned that when God speaks we move forward and stand on His word despite what the circumstances would say. We do the possible and God does the impossible.

As we said yes to renting the new building, we needed a new name for the property then the "Peach House." At the time God was speaking to Adam and me a lot about Psalm 23. *"The Lord is my shepherd I shall not be in want…"* Plus the house number was 23 of that street. That was significant. We called the house 23.

Names have meaning and are significant. That's why changing from "The Peach House" to something more significant was so important to us. So that was why we prayed and changed it. We also felt our base needed another significant name change. When we first had the word in June of 2017 that it was all a go for us to pioneer a base in Paris Adam and I immediately knew we needed a name! We couldn't just be YWAM Paris as there was another YWAM work in the city. So we felt we needed to be YWAM Paris *something*.

Adam talked to one of his elders and they suggested YWAM Paris Central, as our heart was to reach the centre of Paris and the whole city so why not central. Adam brought that to me and we prayed and felt positive about it. It was our heart to reach the city and flowed well.

Yet, after a few months of discussion with various people we decided that it would be wise to change our name to something more inclusive. We didn't realize when we first decided on the name that it could sound exclusive. This wasn't the message we wanted to send. So we went back to prayer for a few months and processed with God, waiting for a new name to come.

We felt quite attached to the acronym YPC so we knew we were searching for a YWAM Paris C-something. We went through a lot of C's and not a lot was sticking with us and it took time to put brain power towards it in the midst of moving and pioneering. But one leaders meeting Adam and I brought to Thierry and Beth a list of five "C" words that could work well with our call and vision.

We then took these to prayer and soon we felt quite certain from Jesus on one. Connect. Connect fit very well and communicated our heart to be a base that connects with others in the city and in the world. YWAM Paris Central officially became YWAM Paris Connect.

The following staff meeting we announced the name change to the base. We then all waited on the Lord together to get words about our new title. Soon the staff were all sharing back positively about what God was saying about the name! It was significant and fit us so much better than Central. It took some time and work to change our website and logos around and emails, but it was worth it as we launched into our new name.

We originally thought April would be a busy month with running the Music DTS and setting up our new base. However, it turned into an even busier month as we rented a new building, announced a new DTS, and gained a new name!

To the human eye it seems insane, but with the word of the Lord over all of it we felt a sense of confidence and assurance that God was still moving in and through all of this. We knew He would make a way for us like He always does.

April ended well, with many new questions and many new to do lists—but we were ready for it.

MAY

"Mercies are new every morning, great is thy faithfulness…
Because of the Lord's great love we are not consumed, for his
compassions never fail. They are new every morning; great is your
faithfulness."
Lamentations 3:22-23 (NIV)

May started beautifully with a push for breakthrough in
multiple areas. We needed a deposit for 23, to see the Frontline
DTS pioneered, and we were gearing up for the two week Paris Je
t'aime event in the summer! So lots to prepare and to see
breakthrough on.

I was in full office mode and using my research skills to see
our office set up with more tables and to get decor for the base so it
wasn't just white walls everywhere. I looked up plants and was
really into this free website as I started getting some free items for
the base. My mom trained me well from years at garage sales and
second hand stores to find a good deal and a bargain. Soon we had
office tables and chairs (all second hand and a good deal of course)

and shelves to put around the base and add more storage for everyone.

The other big adventure and a whole new area for me was setting up our kitchen! When we moved into the base the kitchen was just an empty room that we called the kitchen.

As a base we didn't own any kitchen items except for one freezer we bought for €30 and an oven! We were cooking for 30 people and the kitchen was preparing simple meals with the basics we had. It was hard work but they were doing so well!

Adam and I decided to get a professional kitchen piece by piece. All stainless steel tables and large scale cooking items and we needed a sink! We were doing dishes in the upstairs bathroom sink - which was not convenient at all. I researched and contacted many people about their items and trying to find good prices on it all.

Finally piece by piece we bought a big double sink and had it installed so we could wash dishes! That was exciting for all of us!

Then we bought a 6 element stove top oven and we sent two of our staff two hours away to buy it.

When we got it back its electronics didn't work with the plugs we had at the base so we couldn't use that for a couple of weeks until we had a kind YWAMer from another base who was an electrician and helped us make it work! One of the best pieces we bought was called "Buffalo Bill."

I've only seen these in movies at burger joints or on the streets at kebab shops, the big flat grill which was named Buffalo Bill by someone on our base. This item was my all-time favourite.

Being in YWAM for over ten years and in our kitchens we were constantly frying meat or onions or something and using frying pans and destroying them to now have a giant iron hot plate that turns on and cooks thirty hamburgers at once makes me very happy. It's made for large scale kitchens and means we don't have to keep buying frying pans and them getting destroyed - which would happen oh so much. Buffalo bill was professional and would last a long time!

These little details of our make me happy. The students and staff also use buffalo bill to make eggs on in the morning and it's just so nice having a nice working grill. Soon after we bought big tables and stainless steel cupboards and air vents and our kitchen came together.

It looked so professional! No one would have guessed we bought each item piece by piece. We were ready for cooking and preparing for receiving a hundred more people in July!

One Friday morning worship time, we waited on the Lord and asked God if we personally can give anything towards the financial need for 23. We were trusting for €30,000 to come in. We needed €20,000 for our deposit and the first two months of rent and then another €10,000 for renovations.

A former doctor's office, 23 had plenty of sinks and toilets but no showers. The bathroom renovations needed professional work plus we had to buy bunk beds and mattresses and set it up as a functioning home. So we were trusting for the €30,000. In this time of worship, we felt to share it with the base and invite everyone to hear from the Lord and see if there's anything the Lord would ask them to contribute.

So we waited on the Lord and soon people came forward and were writing down the amount they were to give and as we totalled the amount given within fifteen minutes we saw €18,000 come in!! It was unbelievable!

We were thinking a couple hundred or thousand at most as we were a group of YWAMers. But God just out poured over us and we saw over a third of what we needed come in. It was incredible and we celebrated. Thank the Lord.

It also brought a great level of confidence for me and the leadership team. It was a large risk taking on another building financially and trusting for all that we needed to set up this YWAM base.

As the worship time ended and the Music DTS went to class and all our staff went and did their various jobs, I just say amazed and felt a deep sense of assurance.

God is with us in this, I thought. I know He was all along, but sometimes you have this little thought at the back of your mind like, *What are you doing? Starting an YWAM base and growing so quickly? That's not how this works, are you doing it in your own strength?.*

It's true, some of my fears have been to stay quiet and not grow big or be seen because I don't want other YWAM bases or people to be looking down on us. It happens! Especially in Christian circles, we can be ruled by our insecurities and comparison.

I remember when I went to a DTS meeting and one base was struggling for students on their DTS's and they asked how many I had and I said, "…uhh…we are looking like we are going to have…uh…forty people on the upcoming DTS." I couldn't lie! This was actually what happened in 2017. I have this insecurity of not belonging and not being liked. It all comes from my people pleasing.

So my fear of growing so big so quickly and looking like a "show off" causes me to pull back on what God is actually doing!

It's horrible. It obviously comes from pain in my past. I was teased for being the favoured one or excelling at things differently to my siblings. It caused a distance and a sense that I didn't belong. So I stopped excelling, and I tried to be like them so I could fit in.

I've worked a lot of that out, but there is still a lot there! My fear of man and fear of rejection by my peers can cause me to want to slow down and not be seen. But that is not my call.

God rebuked me one time so strongly when I said to God I wanted to just serve in the background for my life and not be seen or at the front and He said, "Leah you need to lay down your right to not be seen. Lay down your right not to lead."

Obedience is key in this mission. Without it, we are fools running around trying to do things for God and not with Him. So of course I obeyed.

Now I am a leader and leading a YWAM base in Paris and need to again tell myself, my insecurities, my desire to be liked and belong to sit down and not let that get away of God doing what

God wants to do with us. I've learned I need an audience of one; God and God alone.

If God wants our base to grow big and do great things with Him then so be it. Who am I to get in the way of this!? Who cares if people see us and notice how quick we grow.

It's not about us. It's about giving glory to God for what He is doing.

Comparison and fear of man will always hold us back from freely doing what God has called us to do. I don't want that to rule me. So having this large amount of finances come in in fifteen minutes wasn't really about the finances for me. It was God saying to me,

"Leah, I've got you and move on my momentum and what I have for you and not your own."

And that's where I respond, "Yes sir, yes sir, three bags full, sir."

I love Jesus; I love how He knows me and knows what I need, which sometimes is a kick in the pants. Because I love what I do. I love growing. I love making an impact on this city and the nations of the world! I don't want my fears to hold us back from doing this!

So my desire is to be like that quote in Robin Hood (not the cartoon one, the one with Russell Crow), "Rise and rise again until lambs become lions." We are called to be lions: to advance and move forward the kingdom of God. Not to be lambs that follow what everyone else does. I want to stand out for being a woman who fears the Lord and not a woman who looks like everyone else. Rising to who God has called me to be which is strong and courageous with Him.

When the money came in for 23, we were able to move forward on getting the building ready and equipped for receiving teams! The big job was getting showers installed. Adam and Thierry and I met to strategize. This was a whole new area for us. Adam thought we could install the showers and do the plumbing ourselves; but for me there was no way we could handle that. So Thierry was commissioned to get some quotes for us.

One quote came back that was way over what we could afford. That got us worried. How do we do this? Then a student from Paris mentioned that she knew of a plumber who installed her family's home shower. She contacted the plumber. He met with Thierry, gave us a good quote and within ten days we had six new showers installed into 23!

It was coming together just in time for our teams arriving back in June! We also ordered bunk beds and mattresses as 23 had enough rooms to house around forty five people! We worked hard at getting it all ready!

It was dorm style living, but the house would work well for the more short term teams coming in and out. As well, it worked for some of our long term staff as well. God was faithful in every area for us! We didn't even have to do a big financial ask to see all the finances come in. God in his kindness and faithfulness brought release for us to move forward and get the building ready for the new DTS and the upcoming Paris Je t'aime.

Our three teams on outreach were doing well. I was in regular communication with the teams and how their locations were and how the teams were going. It was mostly positive; there are always more discipleship problems on outreach that need to be worked out. You see how a person truly is when they are in high pressure situations. Like a fruit, when they are squeezed their real juices come out. It's a good self-analysis: when I am squeezed, what comes out? Pressure reveals the real me. How do I respond?

I was hearing different reports of how various team members were being squeezed and I needed to help bring correction and teach people where they were wrong. The different teams had different problems and even in some of the locations they were doing ministry, looking at the problems within the ministry and the schedule and seeing where we can change.

It depends where we send the teams, but some locations there is nothing set up for ministry and this is more of a creative outreach. For others there every breath and break is scheduled and this is more of a "submit and serve" role but can also take a toll on the team if they have no time together and no time to debrief. This was happening with some of the teams and something that we had to quickly remedy as the teams were getting exhausted and needed time to breath. But that's the beauty of being sent from a base, to have someone to reach out to and be out of the situation and to course correct where things can get off.

God was faithful in His dealings with the team and all three teams came through it all beautifully. They saw amazing things happen with God and were lead in all their locations to see people know about God more.

Outreach is essential in our mission: to reach out, to do evangelism, and to see impact.

The truth really does set people free and the truth is Jesus. It is confronting doing evangelism every day on outreach and it causes people's pressure juices to come out. But the end result is someone knowing more about God! It's powerful because when you do evangelism and you meet someone and pray for them, they then know they are not alone and that they are loved and have purpose. That is what this world needs!

People need to know that they are special and have something to live for other than themselves. We as Christians have the truth, aka Jesus, and we have such great opportunity to share Him wherever we go. That's why DTS outreaches are so impacting because the whole purpose of the outreach is evangelism—to tell people everywhere they go about Jesus. The change and the transformation we see in people is unexplainable.

That's why we do what we do. It is hard and it can be tiring, but for another person to know the truth it is worth it. That is why as a base we do weekly evangelism—it gets us out of ourselves and our comfort zones and again reminds us it is not about us!

We were also invited to take part in the March For Jesus at the end of May. The March for Jesus was an international annual event where churches and Christians march down the main roads of their cities as a declaration of their faith in Jesus. The event has mostly died out in many cities.

It reached its peak in the early 90's and the main theme song was the famous "Shine Jesus Shine." For some reason France has held on to the tradition of March for Jesus and it is still going strong in many of their main cities!

For me, the March for Jesus holds a significant memory. When I was a child, before my parents divorced, we participated in the March for Jesus. I remember being on my dad's shoulders and with all our other church friends and celebrating and singing our love for Jesus. As a child I remember being so happy and delighted to go to the streets and show our love for Jesus. It is also one of the only strong memories I have of my parents proclaiming their love for Jesus.

So for me participating in the March for Jesus in Paris was significant as it held the emotions of me as a younger time, when things were less complicated.

When the day of the event came all of us YWAMers made our way downtown and found our place in the procession. It was a far greater event then we anticipated! There were thousands of people all over the street wearing March for Jesus shirts and waving flags! There were colours and cultures and multiple nations!

They also had bands situated upon the backs of eight semi-trucks. The semi-truck backs were open and these bands were not quiet! It became a dancing, singing, marching proclamation of truth! I loved it!

I was no longer a child on my father's shoulders but now marching my own journey for Jesus. Us YWAMers all gathered behind the Semi-Truck where our YWAM band was asked to play. We walked a good couple hours through the streets of Paris and ended in the centre of the city at Republique. God was present. It was a day not easily forgotten, especially in days where most marches or city demonstrations were opposing to God and His ways.

We finished the month of May feeling more settled. With one DTS on outreach and the Music DTS in its eighth week of lectures, we felt settled. We didn't have to worry about moving in two months time and the kitchen was fully functioning and our base just clicked over like clockwork. People knew their roles and we moved forward in being established and setting up more systems.

God's faithfulness remained as we moved into June and into our next battles ahead with a new quarter.

JUNE

"So is my word that goes out from my mouth: It will not return to me empty but will accomplish what I desire and achieve the purpose for which I sent it. You will go out in joy and be led forth in peace the mountains and hills will burst into song before you and all the trees of the field will clap their hands."

Isaiah 55:11-12 {NIV)

At the beginning of June, Adam and I moved into our renovated apartment. We finally had a home.

This was a huge relief for us from living out of bags for seven months. Our last five years in Biarritz we had moved every single year. This apartment being a three-year contract we felt we could fully make it our home. We were excited. I was ready to decorate, unpack our bags, and set up home. We got a new bed and new furniture and settled in well.

One of our Backpack Europe DTS teams came back early and helped us clean, paint, and set up 23. It was a huge help as we needed to get ready for an outreach team arriving from Kona that was going to be staying with us for six weeks.

Also, the Paris Je t'aime numbers were getting to be over a hundred people coming to stay with us. Having the outreach team with us was a big help. They painted 23 with a fresh coat of paint, built all the bunk beds we ordered, and set up the rooms in time for the Kona team that arrived at the end of June.

We also had our first DTS graduation as YPC! There were a lot of firsts in our first year but running and graduating our first DTS was a big accomplishment for us. We had a week of debrief for all the teams. It was a time to process the last six months and also to prepare all the students to re-enter back into their home life.

This is often a large transition for people who do a DTS. Each person is taking six months away from their normal life to grow and go deeper with God and have a cross-cultural mission's experience. It's challenging but also rewarding as the students lay down selfishness and hard hearts to take on the role of serving and helping others in the nations. They all go through such deep personal change and make some of the deepest friendships they have ever had.

So transitioning out of living and being surrounded with people constantly for six months to go home to your own room and food and life can be hard...especially for people going back to difficult situations or not having a supportive network.

We have to prepare them that just because they went through deep life and heart change doesn't mean that everyone has. For everyone else, life has continued.

The graduation was fun. We even had an open mic and different people performed. Two days later they left us, taking flights and trains back to their hometowns with vision and purpose from God.

I said goodbye to Levi again, but it was so exciting to see that God was calling him to continue in YWAM and do a second level school with YWAM called the School of Biblical Studies. I was thrilled as God was leading him strongly. He had a few months at home to prepare before he went to do that school in Australia.

We said goodbye to all twenty of them and blessed them as they go. A few of them we would knew we would see them again as some felt to come back and join us for two years on staff.

The next week we had the commissioning night for the Music DTS. They were about to head out on outreach, and we commission each of our teams as they go. We lay hands on them, pray for them, and send them out to see great things happen to all the places they go.

The music DTS split into two teams but for the first four weeks they were going to be all together. They spent the first two weeks at the Montreaux Jazz Festival in Switzerland performing and evangelizing to the people there. The latter two weeks were with us in Paris for the Paris Je t'aime. They helped with setup, evangelism and performing as well.

After that one team headed to the Middle East and the other team went to Albania, Montenegro, and Kosovo. Each team had different connections in each location and either joined alongside another ministry or church or YWAM base to help and serve.

The more we send teams out and the more I am in missions I see that everywhere we go people are hungry and in need of hope. There is so much pain and suffering and hopelessness at times and people want to know answers of why and what's the point. I've seen that just by small gestures of simply going up to someone and saying "God sees you knows you and loves you" can make all the difference in someone's life.

You know when you get the tug in your heart or spirit to go talk to someone on the street? Those are those moments to listen and obey and go and encourage someone. To bring life and value to someone. Often we can think that it's just us or we let our fear of man come in thinking 'what if they laugh at me or reject me.' But we don't know what our obedience does to that person. That person at that moment could be praying and asking God for help or for an answer and we are to be the hands and feet of Jesus to everyone around us.

So we send our teams out and we teach them to respond to the whisper of the Holy Spirit and to love on the lost and the broken. To be ones that are moved with compassion the way Jesus was moved with compassion. When we move in compassion miracles follow. So we commissioned them and off they went excited, ready, and expectant to be used by God.

During the month of June, God spoke to me about fasting for the breakthrough for the Frontline DTS. It was a clear word to run the school, but we hadn't seen much movement on students or numbers.

I put up a Facebook advertisement and wrote a lot of people and places but wasn't seeing breakthrough. Then God said to do the Daniel Fast for three weeks to see students come. So that's what I did. I prayed every lunch hour to trust God for the workers.

The verse that kept coming to me was in Matthew 9:37-38 (NIV), *"The harvest is plentiful but the workers are few, so ask the Lord for the harvesters."*

As a base we started pushing in prayer and asking God for the release for the DTS. This DTS was significant because we were specifically targeting people who have never heard the gospel before. There are over seven billion people in the world and over three million people have never had opportunity or ability to even hear the name Jesus or know the truth of the gospel.

It's one of the greatest injustices in the world today that people don't have a bible in their own language and ability to know their Lord and saviour. Our heart for this DTS is to begin to reach the lost and go to targeted nations where missionary work is illegal or not common.

A long time staffer of ours had a heart for the Middle East and for the unreached. We prayed as leaders and felt it was right to ask her to take on this DTS and lead it for the next number of years. I would lead it with her for this first one and then in the coming years she would lead it herself. She prayed herself and got a yes.

God was knitting the whole thing together. We were trusting for students and it wasn't until a bit into June we received our first serious application! We received this students name in a prayer time. Someone contacted him and invited him to come and he came! There was another girl visiting the base at the time as a guest and soon she also felt God was leading her to do the DTS. At the end of June, we only had two confirmed students for the DTS starting in days.

We had to start the DTS in faith and trust that God would release more students.

JULY

"He said to them, 'Go into all the world and preach the gospel to all creation.'"

Mark 16:15 (NIV)

Oh July…what a month that was. On top of pioneering and trying to run a base, we were starting our first DTS in July, and running the two week evangelical outreach with a total of around 130 people!

I thought, *What are we doing? Only nine months earlier we had arrived in Paris and now we are doing what!?*

This was not in our original five year plan. We'd actually had a five year plan—I think running the Paris Je t'aime and starting an unreached DTS was planned for 2019 and 2020! It's crazy to think that God was leading us in this incredible momentum.

Momentum was my word for the season. God gave it to me when I was questioning how fast everything was going.

God said, "Leah I want you to move at my momentum and not your own."

That scared me but also gave me an incredible amount of confidence. It scared me because what the heck does moving at God's momentum look like? And was this just the beginning of His momentum? Or was there a whole lot more!? It gave me confidence because the one who was saying it was the one who was in charge and has all capability and strength to make this all happen.

So my conclusion was, "Ok." I shrugged my shoulders and moved on, "Let's do your momentum, God!"

July started hard. It tested my faith and patience. God had spoken for us to run the Frontline DTS. In all my prayer times, God spoke about people coming—an army that would go for Him and go to the lost and the unreached. The unreached is extremely on the heart of God so our prayers were fighting for people to respond to the heart of God and reach those who don't know him!

When the Frontline DTS started we had two students. There was more that God wanted to bring, but we weren't seeing the breakthrough. People just weren't joining. We even had many people say they would come and even multiple people apply to come! But there was no follow through.

It was hard for me to have this happen in the midst of fighting in prayer and the words coming through that God had people for this school. One day God said to me,

"Leah, people have free will. I can't force them to come."

God did have more people on His heart to do this school and to be radical risk takers for Christ, but only few were willing to be like the disciples that dropped their nets and left everything behind to follow Him. Too many times I heard the excuses like…

"When I have more money I will go."

"Once I get married, I'll do missions."

"I'll finish education first, then come."

So many excuses in our day and age. Money, marriage, education...none of which are bad, but I look at the responses of the disciples when Jesus said, "Follow me."

They IMMEDIATELY dropped their nets and left everything behind to follow Him.

There was even one man that came up to Jesus and said, "Jesus I will follow you, but first let me bury my dad."

Basically saying let me wait till my dad dies and then I will follow you. Yet Jesus's response was, "Let the dead bury their own dead."

Come on Jesus! Such a boss! If I would say that to these DTS enquiries or the parents who have issues with their son or daughter joining staff, I would get in some crazy trouble.

Why have we become so soft to the radical ways of God? There are people in need and God calls us to GO. Yet, so many people do not go. Something has to change in the area of missions and people leaving everything to follow Him. God's heart is burning for men and women to actually sell everything and follow Him.

One Sunday afternoon I was home alone praying, and I just broke down crying. I felt God's heart for people and for missions. The scripture for the Frontline DTS was "How will they know unless we go?" That truth echoes in the heart of God.

I was crying out for God to move on people's hearts to respond to the call to missions. To give their lives for what Jesus gave his life for—people. I do believe the time is now and I'm praying that we see an influx of change and more people going out to serve, to help and to proclaim.

The school started and by the third week of the school, two more students had arrived! They were both last minute enquiries and applications, but they came! So the Frontline DTS was set with four students and four staff.

We were a unique group of people from so many different backgrounds but we knew from the beginning that God was pulling this group of people together for a reason.

"Small but mighty," was always in my head. We may be small but we can do mighty things for God.

Like Gideon's army in the bible. Gideon was a part of the weakest tribe in Israel and Gideon was the weakest in his family. But the Lord chose him and spoke to him to do great things in His name! The best is when God told Gideon that his army was too big and God wanted to use a small number to defeat the enemy. Gideon had his small army and saw amazing things happen for God. I felt it was the same for the Frontline DTS—small but mighty—just like Gideon's army.

The Paris Je t'aime started extremely well. Way better than I expected, to be honest. It was a lot of work to organize a two week outreach on its own, but then on top of that taking care of accommodation, food, and meetings for a hundred and thirty people for two weeks—that's a lot. Somehow God's grace and wisdom and also our incredible staff team pulled it off!

Each morning we would meet all together at our base auditorium (in the hot summer heat) an hour of worship or prayer to start the day. From there we would have one hour of teaching on

146

evangelism or missions or how to hear God's voice. Then, within fifteen minutes, the auditorium would change into a dining hall so we could all sit down and have our lunch meal together.

After lunch and a break, we grabbed our packed dinners and people broke up into several different evangelism teams across Paris. We had a team that went to love on refugees, another team handed out bibles, another team did kids ministry, and another did preaching on the metro system!

After a few hours doing that all around the city, we would come together around 6pm at a big square in central Paris for a giant evangelical performance. For the first week we were in a square called Republic. It's a popular place in Paris where a lot of demonstrations and performances happen and a lot of people congregate there.

The first week went incredible. We had a good sound system and a stage. Each evening we had amazing Christian performers that came from around the world to be a part of this event. They danced, sang, and did skits.

It was amazing to see nations coming together to give their time and talent for free so that people could know about Jesus. Their performances were not about them being known—it was about others knowing about Jesus.

After a few songs or a performance, someone would give a testimony or preach about the Gospel. Usually we would get a massive crowd anywhere from a hundred to four hundred people. They gathered to watch the performances, but would often stay and listen to the message. A lot of us would watch the performance as well and when the person finished their testimony or preaching we would turn to the person next to us and begin a conversation with them about God or we asked if they needed prayer.

So many people deal with loneliness and hopelessness. It's incredible when you stop and value people enough that they want to share with you and get prayer.

Evangelism does work. Especially when the approach is kind with a genuine desire to see people know Jesus.

The second week of the Paris Je t'aime we had permissions to set up our stage and performances in front of the Eiffel Tower. I've had a lot of amazing moments in my missionary career, but this was one of my highlights.

It was our first year running this event and here we were with permission to set up a stage with sound directly in front of the Eiffel Tower and spend a couple hours performing and telling people about Jesus! It was incredible!

Every evening was a magical time, as a hundred Christians gathered in one of the most popular destinations in the world to preach and tell people about Jesus Christ. Each day, as the sun set and the moon came out behind Eiffey, the tower would sparkle for us to end our evening. People would be finishing praying for people and sharing the love of God all around the famous square, and Eiffey would wrap up our day with a special performance of her own.

It was amazing that God used us. I remember sitting there in awe as Eiffey was sparkling before me and just saying thank you to Jesus. It is not a sacrifice to live for Him; it is a privilege.

Especially moments like this. What a joy it is to follow and know Jesus.

We ran hard for those two weeks as YPC. Our staff was tired, and organizationally we were spent. It was that good tired you get when you do something worthwhile. It takes all your effort and when it's over, but in the end you say to youself, "Wow…we just did that and I am so glad we did…but let's have a break before we do it again."

That kind of feeling.

It was an amazing event and God's hands were all over it! From the accommodation working out, to feeding a hundred and thirty people three meals a day, to organizing teams and a two-hour performance each evening! It was incredible and we were happy with how it all went. Over the two weeks we saw the following things happen:

Statistics from Paris Je t'aime

Salvations: 40

Healings: 42

Received Prayer: 703

Heard Gospel: 1,931

Received Materials: 659

Mercy Ministries: 109

It was a worthy event. God really does use the foolish things of the world to shame the wise. As YWAMers we often feel like fools, but fools that see great things happen.

Like William Carey said, "Expect great things from God; attempt great things for God."

That was the story of our year: hoping God was in all of it and expecting great things to happen—which they did.

After the Paris Je t'aime finished, Adam's parents came for a week visit, and we were able to get away for a few nights with them. We hadn't seen them in two years and were excited for some good quality time and rest.

We headed to the west near Normandy and got an apartment for a few days. We ate good food and explored the sites around the area. It was nice being by the sea again but even better to have lovely time with my in-laws.

They are amazing people and have made many sacrifices in releasing Adam to missions and myself as well. If they hadn't released Adam, then there would be no way we would have been pioneering. Our parents deserve honour and recognition for their sacrifice of letting us be radical ones that follow Jesus.

It's not easy for parents to let their kids go, but as they release us into God's hands and it calls blessings come upon them. Their sacrifice doesn't go unnoticed.

It was such a good week, but I did wish we had a bit longer. I hoped we would see each other again soon. Adam comes from an amazing family of believers and such generous and kind people. I am truly blessed.

As Adam's parents left so did July; the crazy month of starting a new DTS and running a major outreach was over. A deep sigh of satisfaction mixed with relief came over our base, as we looked ahead into August. It was time to rest and regroup together.

AUGUST

"The thief comes only to steal and kill and destroy; I have come
that they may have life, and have it to the full."

John 10:10 (NIV)

August was probably our least eventful month in the whole
year. Boring isn't the word, but least eventful sounds appropriate.

We entered into August still feeling tired from the weeks of
Paris Je t'aime. So many late nights and early mornings. So we
cruised into August with ease…we could breathe again and not feel
like we were running at a high pace speed.

Sometimes people can read these stories and think that we
are not taking care of ourselves and not resting enough or whatever.
I love the care of that thinking. But a few years ago God taught me,
and in turn I feel responsible to teach others, that we as
missionaries need to live a sustainable lifestyle.

We are not called to meet every need that we see. If that were the case I am sure I would have been burned out years ago. We are called to a sustainable lifestyle.

There are sometimes seasons of extra tiredness and busyness. But it's not meant to be that was every day of every year. Sabbaths are of the highest priority. We make sure we have one day a week where we do absolutely no work at all.

Normally we operate on a five day schedule and have weekends free to rest and fill our soul with other enjoyments in life besides being a missionary. It's healthy and good. So July was our busy month, but we knew August was coming and so did Jesus. He knew we needed a month to recover and rest and just do normal day to day tasks before we end this quarter and start a whole new year again.

That's what August was…a normal day schedule with great times of worship and prayer.

Our dining hall, which was once sixteen tables filled with chairs and plates, was down to three or four tables each evening.

We seemed small and quiet and it was nice. Card games would readily happen after dinner with one group, while others would go home and watch a movie or go to bed early. It was healthy for us to have a change of pace. If people need more rest, we would give them time off to recover more.

God was also doing something with us internally. We achieved good things in our ministry and our out pouring, but I soon noticed that God was doing some mending and repairing in our hearts and minds in the area of relationships.

Relationships are a huge priority in the eyes of God and having good healthy relationships is the second greatest commandment! We are called to live right with God and right with others.

God was working on our relationships and poking our hearts in areas of codependency, cliques, and inclusivity. Being twenty three people that have come from all different backgrounds and cultures, a lot of us have to learn how to do relationships well.

Since we are full time missionaries it is easy to focus so much on the task and meeting people's needs, that we can make relationships a lesser priority. That just isn't true. The only ability we have to be a successful missionary base is by having good community. We need healthy relationships where we fill each other up. This gives us the ability to pour out.

That is why relationships corporate worship, prayer, and eating two meals a day together are so key. Through this, we become friends, support each other, and from that place of strength, we pour out to people's needs.

I've seen missionaries that have no community and just "Have the mission" and "Complete the task" mentality, and that is when they rely on their own strength and not God's. They don't get strengthened by others. This in turn quickly leads to self-reliance and burn out.

One of YWAM's foundational values is to "Function in Teams." This value of working and living together is vital to creating an effective and long lasting work.

Yes, it would be easier if we didn't make two hot meals a day for our staff. Yes, it would be easier to not sit around the table and have our meals family style. We could just do buffet time and come in between six to seven pm to grab our food. Some bases operate that way. But for Adam and I, the value of family and strengthening one another through community was the key for us to continually pour out.

No man is meant to be an island. We all need accountability and support.

Relationships also sharpen us and teach us about ourselves. My favourite scripture about this is, *"As iron sharpens iron so does one man sharpen another"* Proverbs 27:17 (NIV). The more community we are in the more sharpened we get. The more sharpened we get the more effective we are in ministry and leading and helping people because we get to be challenged in the rough areas of our life and see character growth! Any married person would understand immediately.

Through various conversations, I realized that as women staff we needed an aligning to how we were doing relationships.

158

There were fifteen of us on staff. We needed to come together in love and unity.

With girls there can be this mentality that we all need a "best friend." It leads to comparison and even fighting over who can be number one in each other's lives. It's an unhealthy view that movies and the world can teach us that we need "our person" or "best friend" and that's it. It's a false view that I hear often when I talk to my single staff a lot of the time they say, "I don't have a best friend. This person has that person and this one that and you have Adam, but who do I have?"

We are called to have multiple friends and multiple dynamics in friendships. Out of insecurities people can grab on to one person just so they feel safe and have belonging. But that is unhealthy as well because our belonging and our acceptance comes from Jesus. He is our person—our best friend.

Our identity and who we are as woman come from our God and not from each other.

Yes, friendship is good and we need community, but learning to do it together as women and staff where we support and uplift each other. This is key. Not seeking to only hangout with one person all the time. God was beautifully teaching us in this season about openness and vulnerability.

For some staff where they have been hurt and others not feeling included. From this, we were able to restore relationships and walk in forgiveness and move forward. I love how God works in all of this. He longs that we walk out in right relationships with one another.

Sometimes we can think God is task focused and all about saving the world, but His care and concern for us as his people come down to details and making sure we are ok and taken care of. This is why I love living in community and being called to this lifestyle, I know it's not for everyone; but for me I am so grateful for it.

I thought August was going to finish with ease. The weather was changing from crazy hot to nice mild temperatures. Our evenings and mornings were getting darker and closing in on us. It was starting to feel like the shift of season from summer to fall which was quite nice. I enjoyed it very much. So far, August was what we hoped it would be—restful and relaxing and lots of community time.

But the last few days of August we were feeling as leaders to pray for the gates of our buildings—spiritually and physically.

Being that Aubervilliers was not a safe area, we are aware of the dangers that can come with a lot of people who come and go from our buildings frequently. During a prayer time as leaders, God spoke about protection and our gates— our front gates were broken on all three of our buildings.

Our main base door had never been locked since we moved in. We had been asking the owner to fix it repeatedly. The day after we prayed, the gate was fixed. It was amazing. We felt it was significant. It meant we had a code to enter into our premises. People couldn't just walk in, which would actually happen often. I was happy to have that extra measure of security as I often would be aware that someone could just come in and take items.

However, the evening after the gate was fixed; two people had entered our apartments which house our staff, students, and guests. That night, a laptop was stolen, along with two wallets, an iPhone, headphones, and two push scooters.

We found out the next morning. It was shocking and emotional especially after our prayer time and having the new code installed on the door! The door lock mechanism had worked for only one day before it stopped clicking shut. People didn't realize that it wasn't actually fully locking. It was no one's fault, but it was sad none the least.

We had worship the morning that it happened. It was a Friday morning, and I announced the incident to the rest of our staff. I read out Psalm 23. It that was what was sticking out to me that morning.

Our staff responded well. We started worshiping, fixing our eyes on Jesus. During worship God gave me an image from the story "How the Grinch stole Christmas." When the Who's all woke up on Christmas morning and all their items were stolen, they didn't whine or complain or get angry. Instead, they all joined together and sang songs and were grateful for what they did have.

It was a powerful image and made me cry. I prayed it out during worship and that's what we did. We didn't focus on what was stolen. We focused on what we did have, which was so much when it comes down to it. We have Jesus and life with Him. He was our source of life and comfort and not possessions. It was an amazing worship time of surrendering ourselves to God and giving Him praise and thanksgiving even in the midst of injustice.

In John 10, Jesus talks about being the good shepherd and that the enemy seeks to steal, kill and destroy, but He came so that we would have life and life to the fullest!

That is our heart's cry. Even when the enemy seeks to steal we would learn to dance upon injustice. We bought new locks and installed more security measures on all of our buildings to avoid any more unwanted guests or theft. We recognize that our battle isn't against flesh and blood but spirit and principalities. The police were informed, but there was not much else we could do.

We forgave the men who took our things and we moved forward, without fear, into all the things that God had for us as a base.

SEPTEMBER

"Now faith is confidence in what we hope for and assurance about what we do not see."

Hebrews 11:1 (NIV)

Our 11th month as a base.

This was a big month: Music DTS was ending, Frontline DTS was being sent on outreach, and we were having our first staff retreat as YPC! It was also the last month of our first year of pioneering.

Soon we would be in our second year! Being in our second year as a base sounds so much more official than just our pioneering year.

God was speaking about our second year of pioneering being about establishing. Establishing systems and organising better as a home and a functioning base.

By week nine of the Frontline DTS, God said to step out of the classroom and let Emily, the DTS co-leader who I was training to take on the school, lead the rest of the lecture phase. A lot of base decisions had to be made and being in class every morning and carrying the school were limiting my time to be able to work on things as a base.

As I stepped back from the school, God spoke to Adam and I about getting more structure and development on the base. The last ten months we were literally treading water and trying to stay afloat and now was the first time that we actually were able to look at our systems and start to develop them.

There was need to set up our backbone ministries better and to train up our leaders. We also still hadn't set up 23 well. There were couples rooms that just had mattresses on the ground. So I was researching again for more furniture and new pieces to keep making our base a home and not like a hostel. Adam and I have similar taste in decor, which makes decisions on buying new furniture and decorations quite easy. We like a clean simple look with a few splashes of colour. Both of us started decorating the base again and arranging systems. Things we loved doing!

God also spoke about getting a bookshelf and ordering books from YWAMers and other leadership books! We want to develop our staff: to keep teaching them and discipling them into the leaders they are called to be. We bought a book shelf and put in a book order.

One of our biggest lessons that we ourselves know and we keep teaching, is to stay teachable. We can always learn. We need to always be ready to learn no matter what the situation. Humility is key in learning. To imitate Christ's humility (Philippians 2) is something I often teach on and often cry out for in my life. We want to be a base that isn't just doing what we think is right, but submitting to God and humbling walking out in who He has called us to be. Humility is essential in leadership as Jesus is the greatest leader and He is the most humble. This was Adam and my cry as we lead this work.

September was a difficult month for Adam and I on a personal level. It's a part of our story that I debated about putting in this book because it has been a long process. There was so much to tell and explain, but I felt the little nudge from God to mention it.

Adam and I have been trusting to get pregnant for several years. Throughout this whole pioneering year, we were going to doctors appointments and having fertility treatments done. It was all in the midst of trusting for buildings and schools and the details of leading a base. It was hard and exhausting, but all of it was in the hopes of being able to have children.

The beginning of September we thought we were going to have some good news to move forward on IVF. Instead our doctor's meeting resulted in me needing to have a surgery and more painful tests before we could try IVF. There were other medical problems as well for of us. It just would take months of more time. It is hard to hear especially in a place of trusting for such a long period of time and seeing so many breakthroughs in other areas—to hear for us personally that we need to keep waiting and persevering was hard.

It has been seven years of waiting to get pregnant. Seven years of trusting. There have been some good days and some bad days. It's not always easy, but our consistent words from God, encouragement from Him, and remaining loyal to His character were a key for us to stay faithful in the season of waiting. I know that God is in the waiting. I know He will fulfil the promise He has spoken. In the midst of the bad news, I spent time with God. I processed with Him, Adam, and my mentors and I felt refreshed that God will come through. Keep persevering.

By mid-September we had our report back for our Music DTS and we also commissioned our Frontline DTS onto an eight week outreach to Nepal. Our second DTS was finished and our third DTS was heading on outreach! What a year to run three DTS's. We were also looking ahead to our Medical DTS starting the first week of October and then running a Seminar in November.

The seminar was about equipping people in the basics of counselling, debriefing, and crisis response. It was going to be such a tool for us as full time missionaries to have these skills and be more equipped in our long term work.

As a way to end the first year as a base, we went away on a staff retreat for a week. It was incredible. I was trusting God for a big beautiful mansion by the ocean for all of us to go to as a staff group. We worked hard this whole year and taking a week together to be family and come together was so key in refreshing and getting ready for a new year. I had my mind set on something wonderful.

However, as I looked into the different holiday houses to rent, the nice ones were way out of our price range and the ones in our price range were not so pretty and looked more like a dingy motel then a place to rest and retreat. As I prayed God said he wanted to give us something good and the first fruits on the land. Adam was adamant that we needed a pool. So then my mission was a mansion by the ocean with a pool!

While I looked I started writing the more expensive places and would say we could only afford the set amount in our budget. Many wrote back and said no, that they could not go that low. But I kept going. Throughout this year I have seen God provide in so many ways for our accommodation and in the impossible ways. I knew He cared about our staff retreat and giving us something nice.

I wrote more houses, until one house in particular, that was double the amount we could afford, came up. I asked them if they were available for our dates and if we can put more people in the house then they were asking and if we could have it for half the price.

They said yes. We had our mansion, with a pool, by the ocean!

I told the base and we all rejoiced again at God's faithfulness to us. It was becoming normal, if it was possible that miracles can be normal, but they were.

This whole year I counted miracle after miracle. So many things that should have been no, became a yes!

God was God. There's no doubt about it and we saw it so often.

On staff retreat we had a time of remembrance. Remembering all that God has done for us in the year. Each person, one by one shared what they were thankful for. We ended with worship and singing to Jesus how much we loved Him.

I often get reminded of the story of the ten lepers who got healed and only one came back to say thank you,

"One of them when he saw he was healed, came back, praising God in a loud voice. He threw himself at Jesus' feet and thanked him -- and he was a Samaritan. Jesus asked, "Were not all ten cleansed? Where are the other nine? Has no one returned to give praise to God except this foreigner?" Luke 17:11-19 (NIV)

This book is to be a book of remembrance and thanksgiving.

I never want to be like the other nine lepers who quickly got what they wanted and never returned to say thank you. I want to always remember what God has done this year and give glory to Him about the battles that turned into victories.

This year is a giant testimony of the on going faithfulness of God.

He's never let us down.

I am continually amazed at the preciousness of our saviour. That He would use me, and walk this journey with Adam and I. He deserves all the glory, and all the praise in this year, and I am ready for the stories that will continue to come as our years roll on.

EPILOGUE

"Let us run with perseverance the race marked out for us, fixing

our eyes on Jesus."

Hebrews 12:1-2 (NIV)

This is just the beginning, and in no way can share all the greatness that God has done.

It was insane to look back at the previous twelve months and think about all the things that God did. It was easy to forget, or sometimes simplify the miracles, or even rationalize how it all happened. Maybe that is why God pressed on me to write this book and write all the stories down.

I am not a professional writer; not a good one anyway. I think I got a C in English and I don't read books often. I can teach pretty well, but writing with grammar and spelling is not my highest gifting. That is why someone is going to edit this like a boss and we need to thank them for that because we need to remember.

I have written down these stories with the most honesty and truth I can give from my memory. I wrote them all down the best way I knew how to. I know there are many more stories ahead, but this first year was nothing short of a miracle.

One thing I know for sure is that God is real and He is moving in the big and in every detail.

He is not apart from our lives but does life with us—as much as we allow Him to be. When we let Him in and do life with him it's a freaking incredible ride.

Thank you for reading our journey. Hopefully the coming years are an ongoing exciting ride with Jesus. I am sure I won't write a book every year about how we are, but if you want to know more please check out our website or you can write me personally on my email below.

To finish, I want to write the words to my favourite song:

I have decided to follow Jesus

I have decided to follow Jesus

I have decided to follow Jesus

No turning back, no turning back

The world behind me, the cross before me

The world behind me, the cross before me

The world behind me, the cross before me

No turning back, no turning back

Though none go with me, still I will follow

Though none go with me, still I will follow

Though none go with me, still I will follow

No turning back, no turning back

Leah Thompson

www.ywamparisconnect.com

leah@ywamparisconnect.com

Thank you to our YWAM Paris Connect Staff Our First
Year:

Adam Thompson

Jon, Olivia &
Nehemiah Allen

Alice Baxter

Bethany Burnett

Wiam Botma

Chloe Brasington

Emily Cahue

Jaimee Caramay

Jessica Cohen

Matthew Dallanegra

Danielle Dean

Stephanie Gomez

Sarah Hastings

Florent Kabashi

Marllon Maciel

DaNiell Mansfield

Emily Mintz

Thierry Noamessi

Danielle O'Leary

Paloma Rivera

Esteban Sao Bento

Kelsey Jones